BLACK

DAYS

Racism and Riots in the U.S.

By J. L. Betcher

Published by
J. L. Betcher
St. Paul, Minnesota
2024

ISBN: 9798332602870

TABLE OF CONTENTS

A NOTE FROM THE AUTHOR

Dear Reader,

In the fabric of American history, there are threads that bind us together in shared triumphs and struggles, and there are threads that tear at the seams of our nation's conscience. Among these threads are the stories of racial unrest and violent civil incidents that have scarred our collective memory, leaving wounds that still ache with the pain of injustice and inequality.

This book is for you, a well-meaning White adult seeking to deepen your understanding and empathy concerning the plight of Black people in the United States. And it's also for you, a person of any color, race, creed or sexual orientation, if you simply want to learn more about the history of racism and riots in the United States. This book is a journey through American history, where we confront uncomfortable truths and reckon with the legacy of racism that continues to shape our society today.

In the following pages, we will explore thirteen examples of race-motivated riots and violent civil incidents that have profoundly impacted Black communities throughout history. From the ashes of Tulsa's Greenwood District to the streets of Ferguson, Missouri, these incidents serve as reminders of the systemic injustices and deep-seated prejudices that have plagued our nation for centuries.

But this book is not merely a recounting of past tragedies. It is a call to action. As we bear witness to the pain and suffering endured by Black

Americans, we also bear responsibility for our own role in perpetuating systems of oppression and inequality.

After a brief introduction to my background as your author, and a chapter clarifying initial definitions necessary to fully understand the book's narrative, each chapter will guide you through a different episode in our nation's history, shedding light on the underlying causes and lasting consequences of racial violence. Along the way, we will learn new truths, challenge long-held beliefs and confront the ways in which our own privilege has blinded us to the struggles of others.

But we will also find hope in the resilience of Black communities, the courage of those who have fought for justice and the potential for a more equitable future. Through education, empathy and action, we can begin to unravel the threads of racism that bind us and weave a new narrative of equality and justice for all.

As we embark on this journey together, I invite you to approach each chapter with an open mind and a compassionate heart. May we emerge from these pages not as passive observers, but as advocates for change, committed to building a more just and equitable society for generations to come.

Let's all find the next "right thing" we can do to combat racism in America.

With humility and determination,

J.L. Betcher

PROLOGUE
ABOUT THE AUTHOR

As I sit down to write this introduction, I am acutely aware of the privileges that my identity as a White person have afforded me throughout my life. This recognition requires not merely an acknowledgment of surface-level advantages but a deeper understanding of the systemic benefits that come with being part of a majority group in a society structured around racial hierarchies.

My understanding is far from complete. But I continue to expand the depth of my appreciation for this profound advantage in life that my society has granted to me at the great expense of others.

Privilege, particularly White privilege, is an unearned advantage based on race. It manifests in various forms, from subtle social cues to overt systemic biases. As a White person, I have had the luxury of viewing my race as a non-issue in most areas of my life.

I have experienced my White privilege as "normal" life—everything being as expected. I have not had to grapple with the negative stereotypes or prejudices that people of color face daily. This lack of racial burden is a significant form of privilege. Living in racism is a burden in and of itself—a stress that is ever-present and ubiquitous.

Growing up, I rarely questioned why the heroes in my textbooks, the protagonists in the novels I read, and the leaders celebrated in my history classes were overwhelmingly White. This representation assured me, consciously or not, that people who looked like me were inherently successful, intelligent and powerful. I never doubted that I could aspire to these heights because I saw myself reflected in these narratives.

When I walked into a store, I was never followed or scrutinized by staff suspicious of my intentions. When I applied for jobs, I never worried that my name or ethnicity might lead to my resume being discarded before I had a chance to prove my capabilities. When I expressed my opinions passionately, I was rarely dismissed as "angry" or "aggressive." These everyday experiences are privileges I took for granted for much of my life.

Beyond daily interactions, systemic advantages play a crucial role in perpetuating the White privilege from which I benefit. Educational institutions, workplaces and legal systems often operate in ways that benefit White people, intentionally or otherwise. For example, predominantly White neighborhoods frequently receive better funding for schools, leading to a cycle of educational and economic advantages/disadvantages that are difficult to break. In the workplace, networks and mentorship opportunities are often more accessible to those who share racial or cultural backgrounds with existing leadership—people like me—perpetuating a cycle of White dominance.

Recognizing my entitlement as a White person comes with the responsibility to act. It is not enough to acknowledge these privileges; I must use these advantages to advocate for change. This means listening to and amplifying the voices of people of color, educating myself on the history and ongoing realities of racial injustice and challenging the systems and behaviors that perpetuate inequality.

I invite you to join me on this journey. But be ready to experience uncomfortable self-reflection and an unwillingness to confront your own biases and . . . your complicity in systemic racism. Our active participation is required in dismantling the structures that benefit us unfairly. It is about moving beyond guilt or defensiveness and towards meaningful action and allyship.

True equity among races will not be achieved until the privileges I enjoy are accessible to everyone, regardless of race. This result necessitates not only policy changes and institutional reform but also a shift in societal attitudes and values. It requires a collective effort to create a world where one's opportunities and rights are not determined by skin color.

In conclusion, acknowledging my status as an entitled White person is a crucial step towards understanding and addressing racial inequality. It is a call to action to use my privilege in the service of justice and equality. By doing so, I hope to contribute to a society where privilege is no longer tied to race, and everyone has an equal opportunity to succeed. Writing this book is my most recent attempt to exercise my White privilege for change.

CHAPTER ONE
UNDERSTANDING RACISM:
KEY DEFINITIONS

To navigate the complexities of racism in the United States, it is essential to have a clear understanding of key terms and concepts. This chapter serves as a foundational guide, providing concise yet comprehensive definitions of terms used to describe various practices and conditions related to racism. By familiarizing ourselves with these definitions, we can better comprehend the systemic injustices and inequalities that led to much of the race-related unrest described in the following chapters.

DEFINITION: SYSTEMIC RACISM

Systemic racism, as it applies to Black people in the United States, refers to the pervasive and institutionalized discrimination and inequality that is entrenched within societal structures, including laws, policies, practices and cultural norms. This form of racism extends beyond individual prejudice and manifests through various interconnected systems, such as education, criminal justice, housing, employment, healthcare and politics, perpetuating disadvantage and oppression against Black individuals and communities.

Examples of Systemic Racism:

School Funding. Public schools in predominantly Black neighborhoods often receive less funding than those in predominantly White neighborhoods due to reliance on local property taxes, leading to disparities in educational resources and opportunities.

Disciplinary Practices. Black students are disproportionately subjected to harsh disciplinary actions, such as suspensions and expulsions, compared to their White peers for similar infractions, contributing to the school-to-prison pipeline.

Policing Practices. Black individuals are more likely to be stopped, searched, and arrested by police, often due to racial profiling and biased enforcement of laws.

Sentencing Disparities. Black people receive harsher sentences than White people for the same crimes, and the War on Drugs has disproportionately targeted Black communities, resulting in higher incarceration rates.

Redlining. Historically, Black neighborhoods were marked as high-risk areas for mortgage lending, preventing Black families from buying homes in certain areas and building wealth through homeownership.

Rental Discrimination. Black individuals often face discrimination in the rental market, leading to higher rates of housing instability, substandard living conditions and inflated rent costs.

Hiring Practices. Black job applicants frequently experience bias in the hiring process, with studies showing that resumes with traditionally Black-sounding names receive fewer callbacks than those with White-sounding names.

Wage Gaps. On average, Black workers are paid less than their White counterparts for the same work, contributing to a persistent racial wealth gap.

Access to Healthcare. Black communities often have less access to quality healthcare facilities and providers, resulting in poorer health outcomes.

Medical Bias. Black patients are less likely to receive appropriate pain management and other treatments due to implicit biases among healthcare professionals.

Voter Suppression. Black voters face barriers to voting, such as strict voter ID laws, purges of voter rolls and limited access to polling places, undermining their political representation.

Gerrymandering. Racist politicians manipulate electoral district boundaries to dilute the voting power of Black communities, reducing their influence in elections and policymaking.

Conclusion.

Systemic racism is deeply embedded in the fabric of American society, creating and perpetuating inequalities that hinder Black people's ability to achieve equal opportunities and outcomes.

DEFINITION: REDLINING

Redlining is a discriminatory practice that systematically denies services, financial products and opportunities to residents of certain areas based on their race or ethnicity, particularly affecting Black communities in the United States. This practice, historically carried out by banks, insurance companies and government agencies, involved drawing red lines on maps to delineate neighborhoods deemed high-risk for investment, effectively segregating these communities and stifling their economic growth.

Following are some ways redlining has limited opportunities for Black Americans.

Mortgage Denials. Black families were often denied mortgages or offered loans with unfavorable terms, making it difficult for them to purchase homes and build generational wealth.

Property Value Depreciation. Homes in redlined areas were undervalued, leading to lower property values and diminished wealth accumulation for Black homeowners.

Business Loans. Black entrepreneurs faced barriers to securing loans to start or expand businesses, limiting economic development and job creation in their communities.

Infrastructure Neglect. Redlined areas received less investment in infrastructure and public services, resulting in deteriorating schools, parks and public transportation.

School Funding. Schools in redlined neighborhoods were underfunded due to lower property tax revenues, leading to poorer educational facilities and resources.

Limited Opportunities. The lack of quality education impeded the academic and professional advancement of Black students, perpetuating cycles of poverty.

Medical Facility Scarcity. Redlined communities often had fewer and lower quality healthcare facilities and providers, leading to poorer health outcomes and limited access to medical care.

Health Disparities. The stress and economic instability caused by redlining (among other discriminatory practices) contributed to higher rates of chronic illnesses and shorter life expectancies among Black residents.

Pollution and Hazards, Redlined areas were more likely to be located near industrial sites, landfills and other sources of pollution, exposing residents to environmental hazards and health risks.

Green Space Deficiency. These neighborhoods often lacked parks and recreational areas, affecting the physical and mental well-being of residents.

Voter Suppression. The economic and social instability fostered by redlining made it more challenging for Black residents to participate in the political process, leading to underrepresentation and reduced political power.

Policy Neglect. Elected officials were less likely to address the needs of redlined communities, perpetuating neglect and disinvestment.

Long-term Effects. Redlining has had a lasting impact on Black communities, contributing to the racial wealth gap and perpetuating economic and social disparities. Although redlining was officially outlawed with the Fair Housing Act of 1968, its legacy continues to affect Black Americans today, as many of the systemic barriers it created have yet to be fully dismantled.

DEFINITION: RESTRICTIVE COVENANTS

Restrictive covenants are clauses in property deeds or leases that impose limitations or conditions on the use of the property. When related to limiting Black access to real property, restrictive covenants specifically refer to provisions that prohibited the sale, lease or occupation of a property to Black individuals (and often other racial minorities). These covenants were legally binding agreements that were widespread in the United States during the first half of the 20th century and played a significant role in maintaining racial segregation in residential areas.

Deed Restrictions. Property deeds included language explicitly barring Black people from owning, renting or occupying homes. For example, a deed might state that the property could not be "sold, leased, or occupied by any person of the Negro race."

Enforcement. These covenants were enforced by neighborhood associations, homeowners' groups and sometimes local governments, ensuring that Black families were legally prevented from moving into certain areas.

Segregated Neighborhoods. Restrictive covenants were used to create and maintain all-White neighborhoods, confining Black families to designated areas with fewer resources and opportunities.

Economic Disparities. By limiting where Black individuals could live, restrictive covenants contributed to economic segregation, affecting access to quality education, employment and public services.

Court Cases. Some Black families challenged restrictive covenants in court. The landmark case *Shelley v. Kraemer* (1948) resulted in the U.S.

Supreme Court ruling that while restrictive covenants themselves were not unconstitutional, state enforcement of such covenants was.

Civil Rights Activism. Activists and organizations, such as the NAACP, fought against restrictive covenants and other forms of housing discrimination, leading to greater public awareness and legal reforms.

Residential Patterns. The legacy of restrictive covenants contributed to long-lasting residential segregation patterns that persist in many American cities today.

Wealth Accumulation. Because homeownership is a primary means of building wealth, the exclusion of Black families from certain neighborhoods severely limited their ability to accumulate wealth and pass it down through generations.

Community Resources. The concentration of Black families in certain areas due to restrictive covenants often meant that these neighborhoods received fewer investments in infrastructure, schools and services, perpetuating cycles of poverty and disadvantage.

Conclusion.

Restrictive covenants were a tool of systemic racism that legally entrenched racial segregation and inequality in the housing market. Although such covenants were rendered unenforceable by the Supreme Court decision in *Shelley v. Kraemer* and further prohibited by the Fair Housing Act of 1968, their impact is still felt today. The historical use of restrictive covenants has left a legacy of racial disparities in homeownership, wealth and access to quality living environments for Black Americans.

DEFINITION: WHITE PRIVILEGE

"White Privilege" refers to the societal advantages that White people experience solely due to their race, which are often invisible to those who benefit from them but have significant impacts on the lives of Black people and other people of color. In many ways, White privilege is the flip side of the coin to Black disadvantages—a different perspective on the same issues. The advantages of White privilege manifest in various aspects of life, including social, economic, educational and political realms. White privilege is the result of systemic racism and historical inequalities that have positioned White people in a place of relative advantage compared to Black people.

Following are some examples of White privilege:

Employment. White individuals are more likely to receive callbacks for job interviews and promotions compared to equally qualified Black candidates. This privilege results in higher employment rates and better job positions for White people, contributing to economic disparities.

Wealth Accumulation. Historical practices such as redlining and discriminatory lending have allowed White families to accumulate wealth through homeownership, while Black families have been systematically excluded from these opportunities. This has led to a significant racial wealth gap.

School Quality. White students are more likely to attend well-funded schools with greater resources, experienced teachers and advanced programs. This disparity is partly due to property tax funding mechanisms that benefit wealthier (and predominantly White) neighborhoods.

Disciplinary Practices. White students often face fewer and less severe disciplinary actions in schools compared to Black students, who are more likely to be suspended or expelled for similar behavior, affecting their educational attainment and future opportunities.

Policing. White people are less likely to be stopped, searched or arrested by police compared to Black people. This disparity in treatment contributes to higher incarceration rates among Black individuals and a pervasive sense of fear and mistrust towards law enforcement.

Sentencing. White individuals often receive lighter sentences for the same crimes compared to Black individuals, reflecting systemic biases within the criminal justice system.

Neighborhood Choice. White individuals have historically had more freedom to choose where to live, often moving into safer neighborhoods with better amenities and schools. Black families have faced restrictions and discrimination in the housing market, limiting their options.

Home Loans. Even today, White applicants are more likely to be approved for mortgages and receive better loan terms compared to Black applicants, making it easier for White families to buy homes and build wealth.

Access to Healthcare. White individuals generally have better access to healthcare services and facilities. Black individuals often face barriers such as fewer or lower quality healthcare providers in their communities and implicit biases in treatment decisions.

Health Outcomes. Due to better access and treatment, White people tend to have better health outcomes, while Black individuals experience higher rates of chronic conditions and lower life expectancies.

Representation. White people see themselves represented positively in media, education and positions of power, reinforcing a sense of normalcy and belonging. Black people often see negative stereotypes or a lack of representation, affecting their self-image and societal perceptions.

Social Interactions. White individuals are less likely to experience racial profiling or discrimination in everyday situations, such as shopping, driving or applying for housing. Black individuals frequently encounter bias and suspicion, impacting their daily lives and mental health.

Conclusion.

White privilege operates as an invisible system of advantages that benefits White people at the expense of Black people and other people of color. It perpetuates racial inequalities by providing White individuals with unearned benefits and opportunities, while systematically disadvantaging Black individuals. Recognizing and addressing White privilege is essential for creating a more equitable and just society. This involves not only acknowledging the existence of these privileges but also actively working to dismantle the systemic structures that uphold them.

DEFINITION: IMPLICIT BIAS

Implicit bias refers to the unconscious attitudes or stereotypes that affect an individual's understanding, actions and decisions in an involuntary manner. These biases are often rooted in societal norms and cultural practices and can influence behavior without the person being aware of them. When it comes to racial discrimination in the United States, implicit bias plays a significant role in perpetuating inequities and injustices, even among individuals who consciously endorse egalitarian beliefs.

Following are some examples of implicit bias at work:

<u>Hiring Practices.</u> Studies have shown that Employers may unconsciously favor resumes with traditionally White-sounding names over those with Black-sounding names, resulting in fewer job opportunities for Black applicants despite equal qualifications.

<u>Education.</u> Teachers may unknowingly call on White students more often or have lower expectations for Black students, affecting their academic experiences and outcomes.

<u>Policing.</u> Police officers may be more likely to stop, search or use force against Black individuals due to implicit biases, leading to higher rates of police encounters and brutality against Black communities.

<u>Judicial Decisions.</u> Studies have shown that judges and jurors sometimes unconsciously impose harsher sentences on Black defendants compared to White defendants for similar offenses, contributing to racial disparities in the criminal justice system.

<u>Medical Treatment.</u> Healthcare providers may offer different levels of care or dismiss the concerns of Black patients due to implicit biases, resulting in poorer health outcomes and lower quality of care.

<u>Pain Management.</u> Studies have shown that Black patients are less likely to receive adequate pain management compared to White patients, partly due to implicit biases held by healthcare professionals.

Customer Service. Black customers may receive less attentive or courteous service in stores and restaurants due to implicit biases, affecting their overall consumer experience.

Social Perceptions. Implicit biases can lead to the unconscious association of Black individuals with negative traits, such as criminality or aggression, influencing how they are perceived and treated in various social contexts.

Mortgage Approvals. Lenders may unconsciously deny or offer less favorable terms to Black applicants compared to White applicants, contributing to the racial wealth gap and housing disparities.

Rental Markets. Landlords may exhibit implicit bias by favoring White renters over Black renters, even when all applicants have similar qualifications and backgrounds.

Conclusion.

Implicit bias is a subtle but pervasive form of racial discrimination that operates unconsciously, influencing behaviors and decisions in ways that perpetuate racial inequities. By understanding and addressing implicit bias, individuals and institutions can work towards eliminating these injustices.

DEFINITION: RACIAL PROFILING

Racial profiling refers to the discriminatory practice by law enforcement officials, private security personnel or other authorities of targeting individuals for suspicion of crime based on their race, ethnicity or national origin rather than on any individual suspicion or evidence of wrongdoing. In the context of Black people in the United States, racial profiling is a manifestation of systemic racism that results in disproportionate scrutiny, harassment and violence against Black individuals and communities.

Traffic Stops. Black drivers are more likely to be pulled over by police, often for minor infractions or for no specific reason, compared to White drivers. This practice, known as "driving while Black," leads to higher rates of searches, arrests and use of force against Black motorists.

Stop-and-Frisk. Programs like New York City's stop-and-frisk policy have disproportionately targeted Black and Latino individuals, leading to frequent and often humiliating stops, searches and interrogations without probable cause.

Use of Force. Black individuals are more likely to experience excessive or lethal force during encounters with law enforcement. High-profile cases of police shootings of unarmed Black men, women and children highlight this disparity.

Arrests and Incarceration. Black people are arrested and incarcerated at significantly higher rates than White people for similar offenses, often due to racial profiling practices that result in more frequent interactions with the criminal justice system.

Shopping. Black shoppers are often followed, scrutinized or accused of theft in stores, a practice sometimes referred to as "shopping while Black." This can result in unwarranted detentions, searches and embarrassment.

Public Spaces. Black individuals may be more likely to be questioned or confronted by security personnel in public spaces such as parks, malls and neighborhoods, based on assumptions about their clothing, presence or behavior being suspicious.

<u>Profiling by Customs and Border Protection.</u> Black immigrants and travelers are more likely to be stopped, questioned and searched at border crossings and airports due to racial profiling practices.

<u>Psychological and Emotional Toll.</u> Frequent experiences of racial profiling can lead to chronic stress, anxiety and debilitating trauma for Black individuals. It can also contribute to feelings of alienation, distrust of authorities and a diminished sense of safety and belonging.

<u>Community Relations.</u> Racial profiling undermines trust between Black communities and law enforcement, making it less likely that community members will cooperate with police or report crimes, thereby compromising public safety.

<u>Legal and Economic Consequences.</u> Racial profiling can result in wrongful arrests, fines and legal fees, as well as lost wages and job opportunities. The long-term impact includes a criminal record that can permanently affect housing, employment and educational prospects.

<u>Conclusion.</u>

Racial profiling is a pervasive and damaging practice that disproportionately targets Black individuals, contributing to broader systemic inequalities and injustices. Addressing racial profiling requires comprehensive efforts to reform policies, educate law enforcement and build trust with affected communities.

DEFINITION: JIM CROW LAWS

Jim Crow laws were a series of state and local laws enacted in the United States, primarily in the Southern states, in the late 19th and early 20th centuries. These laws were designed to enforce racial segregation and discrimination, particularly targeting Black citizens, and were characterized by strict racial segregation in public facilities, accommodations, transportation, schools and other areas of public life.

Key features of Jim Crow laws included:

Segregation. Jim Crow laws mandated the separation of White and Black individuals in virtually all aspects of public life, including schools, transportation, restaurants, theaters, parks and restrooms. Segregation was enforced through "separate but equal" policies, which claimed to provide equal facilities for both races but, in reality, resulted in vastly inferior conditions for Black individuals.

Voting Restrictions. Jim Crow laws included various measures aimed at disenfranchising Black voters, such as poll taxes, literacy tests and grandfather clauses, which disproportionately affected Black citizens and effectively barred them from participating in the political process.

Social and Economic Discrimination. Beyond segregation, Jim Crow laws also enforced social and economic discrimination against Black people. This included restrictions on employment opportunities, housing discrimination and unequal access to public services and resources, perpetuating cycles of poverty and inequality. Even social interaction between Black people and White people was sometimes prohibited.

Violent Enforcement. The enforcement of Jim Crow laws was often accompanied by violence and intimidation, perpetrated by White supremacist groups such as the Ku Klux Klan and supported by local law enforcement. Lynchings, beatings and other acts of racial violence were used to terrorize and control Black communities, reinforcing the power dynamics of segregation and White supremacy.

The effects of Jim Crow laws on Black people in the United States were devastating and far-reaching, including:

Social Segregation. Jim Crow laws reinforced racial hierarchies and fostered a culture of segregation and racial superiority among White people, while Black people were subjected to humiliation, degradation and social exclusion in their daily lives.

Economic Disadvantage. The segregation of schools, neighborhoods and workplaces limited educational and economic opportunities for Black Americans, perpetuating cycles of poverty and limiting upward mobility.

Political Exclusion. Voting restrictions and disenfranchisement measures disenfranchised Black voters, depriving them of political power and representation and perpetuating White supremacy in the political sphere.

Psychological Trauma. The pervasive discrimination and violence of Jim Crow laws inflicted lasting psychological trauma on Black individuals and communities, contributing to feelings of fear, powerlessness and inferiority that haunted Black people every moment of their lives.

Conclusion.

Despite the abolition of Jim Crow laws following the civil rights movement of the 1960s, their legacy continues to shape racial inequalities and disparities in the United States today. Understanding the history and impact of Jim Crow laws is essential for recognizing the ongoing effects of systemic racism and working towards racial equity and justice in society.

DEFINITION: THE CIVIL RIGHTS ACT OF 1964

The Civil Rights Act of 1964 is a landmark piece of legislation in the United States that aimed to end segregation in public places and banned employment discrimination on the basis of race, color, religion, sex or national origin.

In 1964, despite the Supreme Court's landmark decision in *Brown v. Board of Education* (1954) declaring segregated schools unconstitutional, many Southern states continued to resist desegregation. Following are some examples of segregated schools and districts in the South during that period:

Little Rock Central High School, Arkansas. In 1957, Little Rock Central High School became the focal point of national attention when nine Black students, known as the "Little Rock Nine," attempted to integrate the previously all-White school.

Arkansas Governor, Orval Faubus, opposed the integration and deployed the Arkansas National Guard to prevent the students from entering the school. President Dwight D. Eisenhower intervened by federalizing the Arkansas National Guard and sending the 101st Airborne Division to escort and protect Black students, allowing them to attend classes.

Despite the initial integration, Little Rock continued to resist full desegregation. The school district and city officials employed various tactics to delay and limit integration such as so-called "freedom of choice" plans that ostensibly allowed students to choose which school to attend. However, the real effect of these plans was to maintain segregation by discouraging Black students from attending White schools and vice versa.

Prince Edward County Public Schools, Virginia. In 1959, Prince Edward County closed its public schools rather than integrate, leading to a five-year period during which no public education was available to Black children in the county. White children attended private, state-supported "segregation academies." The public schools were not reopened and integrated until 1964.

New Orleans Public Schools, Louisiana. The New Orleans public school system also remained largely segregated after Brown despite earlier attempts at integration, such as the enrollment of Ruby Bridges at William Frantz Elementary School in 1960. And in 1964, many Louisiana schools were still predominantly segregated.

Clarendon County Schools, South Carolina. Clarendon County was home to *Briggs v. Elliott*, one of the cases consolidated into *Brown v. Board of Education*. Despite the Brown ruling, the county and much of South Carolina continued to operate segregated schools, with token integration efforts that left the vast majority of schools segregated.

Jackson Public Schools, Mississippi. Mississippi was one of the staunchest opponents of desegregation. Jackson's public schools, like those in other parts of the state, remained segregated through a combination of legal maneuvers, economic pressure and intimidation tactics against Black families and civil rights activists.

Protests and Activism. At the same time as the school desegregation conflicts, the Civil Rights Movement was in full swing, with activities ranging from nonviolent protests and sit-ins to marches. Notable events included the Freedom Summer, where activists worked to register Black voters in Mississippi.

Violence and Opposition. Civil rights activists often faced violent backlash, including police brutality, bombings and murders. For instance, the bombing of the 16th Street Baptist Church in Birmingham in 1963 and the murders of three civil rights workers in Mississippi in 1964 highlighted the extreme resistance to desegregation and equality.

Political Climate. President Lyndon B. Johnson, who took office after the assassination of John F. Kennedy in November 1963, played a crucial role in advancing civil rights legislation. Johnson's "Great Society" agenda aimed at eliminating poverty and racial injustice.

Economic Conditions. The U.S. economy in 1964 was generally strong, with post-World War II prosperity still in effect. The middle class was expanding, and consumer culture thrived. However, despite overall economic growth, significant disparities remained between White people and Black people. Johnson's War on Poverty aimed to address these issues through various programs like Medicare, Medicaid and food stamps.

Momentum for the Civil Rights Act. The momentum for the Act was largely driven by the Civil Rights Movement, led by figures such as Martin Luther King Jr., Rosa Parks and many others who fought for equal rights and advocated nonviolent resistance.

Montgomery Bus Boycott (1955-1956). King emerged as a national leader during the Montgomery Bus Boycott, which was initiated by Rosa Parks' arrest for refusing to give up her bus seat to a White person. The boycott lasted 381 days and ended with the Supreme Court ruling in *Browder v. Gayle* (1956) that segregation on public buses was unconstitutional.

Martin Luther King, Jr. In 1957, King co-founded the Southern Christian Leadership Conference (SCLC) to harness the power of Black churches in the fight for civil rights and to organize nonviolent protests.

In 1963, King helped organize the March on Washington for Jobs and Freedom, where he delivered his iconic "I Have a Dream" speech, envisioning a future of racial equality.

Also in 1963, King led a series of nonviolent demonstrations in Birmingham, Alabama, which faced brutal responses from authorities.

History of the Act Itself. Initially Proposed by President John F. Kennedy in 1963, the Civil Rights Bill faced strong opposition, especially from Southern legislators. Among them were: Senator Richard Russell Jr. (D-GA), a leading Southern Democrat and a staunch segregationist, who helped organize a filibuster to block the bill, arguing that it violated states' rights and the principles of federalism; Senator Strom Thurmond (R-SC) a former Democrat who switched to the Republican Party, conducted the longest solo filibuster in Senate history against the Civil Rights Act of 1957 and continued his staunch opposition to the 1964 Act; Senator Sam Ervin (D-NC), known for his strict interpretation of the Constitution, opposed the Civil Rights Bill on constitutional grounds.

The Filibuster. A group of 18 Southern senators (known as the "southern bloc") led by Richard Russell Jr. formed a coalition to filibuster the Civil Rights Bill. Their tactics included extended speeches, procedural delays and efforts to amend the bill to make it less effective.

After Kennedy's assassination in November 1963, President Lyndon B. Johnson took up the cause, leveraging his political skills to push the bill through Congress. Following a lengthy and heated debate in Congress, the Bill was passed by the House of Representatives on February 10, 1964, and by the Senate on June 19, 1964, after overcoming a 75-day filibuster.

<u>Major Provisions of the Act.</u> The Act contained a number of historically important provisions, including:

<u>Title II - Public Accommodations.</u> Prohibited discrimination in hotels, motels, restaurants, theaters and all other public accommodations engaged in interstate commerce.

<u>Title IV - Public Education.</u> Authorized the federal government to enforce desegregation in public schools.

<u>Title VI - Federally Assisted Programs.</u> Prevented discrimination in programs and activities receiving federal financial assistance.

<u>Title VII - Employment.</u> Prohibited employment discrimination by private employers, governments and unions. This title also established the Equal Employment Opportunity Commission (EEOC) to help enforce the law.

<u>Title VIII - Registration and Voting Statistics.</u> Directed the Census Bureau to collect registration and voting data to ensure enforcement of the Act.

<u>Impact and Significance of the Act.</u> The Act was instrumental in dismantling the legal framework supporting segregation and discrimination, leading to significant improvements in civil rights for minorities.

<u>Employment Equality.</u> Title VII, in particular, played a crucial role in promoting equal employment opportunities and combating workplace discrimination.

Enforcement and Legacy. The Act paved the way for subsequent civil rights legislation, including the Voting Rights Act of 1965 and the Fair Housing Act of 1968.

Conclusion.

The Civil Rights Act of 1964 is widely regarded as a turning point in American history, symbolizing a commitment to equality and justice. It addressed deeply entrenched racial inequalities and set the stage for future progress in civil rights.

DEFINITION: BLACK DAYS

The title of this book, Black Days, is employed metaphorically to describe periods of extreme racial violence, unrest and persecution directed against Black Americans in the United States. The phrase evokes the darkness and tragedy of these events, but also the strength, resilience, determination and even triumph of Black communities during such times. Here's how "Black Days" can be contextualized in relation to race riots or persecution riots in the US:

Race Riots. This book sometimes uses the historical term "race riots" to describe the societal violence perpetrated against Black people and the Black people's response. The use of this term is for historical accuracy and is not intended to imply that Black people were primarily at fault or even that Black people shared blame with White people for these civil disturbances.

The Red Summer (1919). The term "Black Days" aptly describes the widespread racial violence that occurred during the Red Summer, where numerous race riots erupted across the country. White mobs attacked Black communities in cities like Chicago, Washington D.C. and Elaine,

Arkansas, resulting in many deaths, injuries (both Black and White) and the destruction of Black-owned property.

Tulsa Race Massacre (1921). The Tulsa Race Massacre represents one of the darkest days in American history. White residents, with the support of local authorities, attacked the prosperous Black neighborhood of Greenwood in Tulsa, Oklahoma. This event, marked by extreme violence, arson and looting, led to significant loss of life and the decimation of what was known as "Black Wall Street."

The Detroit Race Riot (1943). The Detroit Race Riot of 1943, which resulted in the deaths of 34 people and significant property damage, is another example of "Black Days." The riot, characterized by intense persecution and violence against Black residents at the hands of both White mobs and law enforcement, spread chaos and destruction over a period of four days.

The Watts Riots (1965). Triggered by the arrest of a Black man by a White police officer, the Watts Riots in Los Angeles saw six days of violent clashes, arson and looting. The resulting chaos highlighted deep-seated racial tensions and systemic inequalities, marking a period of profound struggle for the Black community.

Darkness and Suffering. The phrase "Black Days" symbolizes the profound darkness, suffering and despair experienced by Black communities during these violent episodes. It conveys the sense of mourning and loss that accompanies such tragic events.

Systemic Injustice. "Black Days" accurately describes race riots and persecution riots by underscoring the systemic racism and injustices that precipitate these incidents. It highlights the broader societal failures that allow such violence and persecution to occur.

Collective Memory. Thinking of these occurrences of extreme societal violence as "Black Days" helps to cement their significance in collective memory, ensuring that the pain and lessons of these historical moments are not forgotten. It serves as a reminder of the ongoing struggle for racial justice and equality.

Conclusion.

The title, Black Days, aptly describes this book's recounting of race riots or Black persecution riots in the US, emphasizing the profound impact of these events on Black Americans and on the nation as a whole. It captures the severity of the violence and persecution, the depth of the systemic racism that fuels such events and the enduring legacy of these tragic episodes in American history. But it also captures the collective strength of the Black community in rising up to defend their homes, and later to defend their civil rights.

CHAPTER TWO

NEW YORK CITY CONSCRIPTION

RIOTS OF 1863

The New York City Conscription (or "Draft") Riots of 1863 were among the most violent civil disturbances in American history. They occurred during the Civil War, from July 13 to July 16, 1863, and were driven by a combination of social, economic and racial tensions. Details of the resulting riots can be found below:

Background

Conscription Act of 1863. By 1863, the Civil War was in its third year, and the Union Army faced severe manpower shortages. Voluntary enlistments had declined, and the Union needed more soldiers to continue the fight against the Confederacy.

In response to the need for troops, on March 3, 1863, Congress enacted The Conscription Act of 1863. Also known as the Enrollment Act, the new law mandated that all male citizens and immigrants who had filed for citizenship between the ages of 20 and 45 were eligible for military service. Men were required to enroll by April 1 and the government created a lottery system to select those who would be drafted.

There were provisions for typical draft exemptions, including physical or mental disability, and certain occupations deemed critical to the home front, such as government officials and certain industrial workers.

However, the Act also contained more dubious provisions, including the condition that drafted men could avoid service by paying a commutation fee of $300 or by hiring a substitute to serve in their place. This clause was highly controversial as it effectively allowed wealthier individuals to avoid military service, leading to accusations that the war was a "rich man's war but a poor man's fight."

On January 1, 1863, President Abraham Lincoln issued a presidential proclamation and executive order declaring that all persons held as slaves within the rebellious states "are, and henceforward shall be free." The Emancipation Proclamation enjoined "upon the people so declared to be free to abstain from all violence, unless in necessary self-defence." [sic]

Note: Interestingly, the Proclamation applied only to states that had seceded from the United States, leaving slavery untouched in the loyal border states: Delaware, Kentucky, Missouri and Maryland.

Also Note: New York State's slaves had been freed some years earlier by the Gradual Emancipation Act of 1799, followed by full freedom for all Black people in 1827 pursuant to The Gradual Abolition of Slavery Act of 1817.

The Emancipation Proclamation alarmed much of the White working class in New York, who feared that vast numbers of newly freed slaves from the South would migrate to the city and add further competition to the labor market.

There had already been tensions between Black and White workers in New York since the 1850s, particularly at the docks, with free Black people, as well as economically strapped immigrants from Germany and Ireland, competed for low-wage jobs in the city.

As an example of extreme workplace tension, on March 6, 1863, mobs of mainly White longshoremen, who for decades had refused to work alongside Black people, began attacking Black workers on the docks. The violence quickly escalated, with White rioters targeting not only workers but also Black-owned businesses and homes, as well as White-owned businesses that employed Black workers or had integrated workspaces.

The longshoremen's riot spread across the waterfront and into nearby neighborhoods. Dozens of Black men were beaten, and there were reports of several deaths, although the exact number is unclear.

It appeared that economic tensions between Black and White works were nearing a zenith. It is in this racially-charged climate that the 1863 riots occurred.

The Riots

The Enrollment Act was highly unpopular overall, and understandably, was especially disfavored among the working class and immigrants. Justifiable feelings of unfairness and persecution boiled into violent resistance on July 13, 1863, the third day of the draft lottery, launching what became known as the New York City Draft Riots. Lasting through much of the day on July 16th, the riots morphed from an initial focus on the Act itself to the persecution of Black people and destruction of Black-owned property.

The rioters, predominantly working-class White men, initially targeted government buildings, such as the Provost Marshal's Office, Police Stations and the Mayor's residence as well as armories and other military-related buildings. However, it took only a matter of a few hours for the predominantly White rioters to turn their violence towards Black people and those associated with them.

Rioters attacked Black neighborhoods, homes and businesses. They lynched several Black individuals, burned down the Colored Orphan

Asylum and attacked abolitionists as well as anyone perceived as sympathetic to the draft or to Black civil rights.

Established less than twenty years earlier, the New York Police Department was overwhelmed by the violence and scale of the unrest. It is estimated that their force numbered only two to three thousand sworn officers at the time. Precise numbers of rioters are unknown, but it is clear rioters outnumbered policemen. More enforcement was needed to quell the rioting.

Ultimately, President Lincoln sent in approximately 4,000 federal troops, some redirected from the Battle of Gettysburg, to take control of the situation. Unsurprisingly, the troops used force to suppress the riots. Less obvious was the troops' use of actual artillery to silence the chaos.

After the troops' arrival on July 16th, it took less than a day to convince rioters to go home—at least for those who still had a home.

Estimates of the death toll from the four days of conflict range widely, but it is generally believed that around 119 (mostly Black) people were killed. Thousands were injured and property damage was extensive.

Immediate Impact

The riots had a devastating impact on New York City's Black community. Many Black residents fled the city, and the Black community's population decreased significantly and immediately as a result. Some estimates assess that as much as one-sixth of New York's Black population fled the city in the days following the riots.

Long-term Effects

The riots yielded both negative and positive long-term effects.

Militarization. As a direct consequence of riots, the federal government increased its military presence in New York City and other Northern cities to prevent future disturbances. This move addressed the inadequacy of the fledgling local police departments to keep the peace in times of chaos. In retrospect, it was also a step toward increased militarization of policing functions—a practice that finds fulfillment in many of today's large city police forces.

Workplace Disparities. The riots also led to efforts to address the plight of the working class, though racial tensions certainly persisted in the workplace. There were increased efforts to improve labor conditions and address the economic grievances of workers. For instance, there was a gradual movement towards recognizing labor unions and their right to organize, which gained more traction in the years following the Civil War (although Black people were typically excluded from most unions until the mid-twentieth century).

Social Welfare Programs. In addition, the federal government and various charitable organizations began to focus more on social welfare programs. Established partly in response to the recognition that economic instability could lead to social unrest, these institutions made modest progress in providing economic relief to impoverished families, including food, housing and other forms of assistance.

Economic Issues. Modern experts and academics often cite the Draft Riots as an example of how economic inequality, racial prejudice and political policies can combine to ignite widespread violence.

The New York riots remain among the largest civil insurrections in American history.

New York City Today

It is impossible trace conditions in today's New York directly to the Draft Riots, but at this writing, the Black community in New York City is diverse and vibrant, contributing significantly to the city's culture, economy and social fabric. However, like many urban centers in the United States, New York City's Black community faces substantial challenges and disparities.

Economic Disparities. Economically, disparities persist in areas such as employment, income inequality and access to affordable housing. While there have been efforts to address these issues through initiatives like affordable housing programs and workforce development initiatives, structural barriers, such as limited access to capital and persistently lower wages, continue to hinder economic mobility for many Black New Yorkers.

In 2024, income disparities between the races are substantial, with median White families receiving an estimated $103,727, while the median Black household received only $58,073.

Education Gaps. Education is another significant area of concern. While there are high-performing schools in predominantly Black neighborhoods, there are also disparities in educational outcomes, with Black students more likely to attend under-resourced schools and face obstacles in accessing quality education. Efforts to address these disparities include initiatives aimed at improving school funding, expanding access to early childhood education and promoting equity in school discipline practices.

Healthcare Disparities. Healthcare disparities also affect the Black community in today's New York City, with higher rates of chronic diseases, including diabetes, hypertension and asthma, as well as disparities in access to healthcare services. Community organizations and healthcare providers are working to address these disparities through initiatives focused on improving access to healthcare, increasing health literacy and addressing social determinants of health, some of which are mentioned above.

Other Efforts. Additionally, issues such as criminal justice reform, police-community relations and affordable childcare remain important concerns for the Black community in New York, with ongoing advocacy efforts seeking to address systemic injustices and promote equity and social justice.

Private Organizations. Private initiatives to close the race gap include efforts to educate non-Black residents concerning "White privilege" and "systemic racism"—terms whose definitions seem frustratingly elusive to many White people. Proper appreciation of these two terms remains essential to healing the relationship between White and Black communities.

Overall, while progress has been made in some areas, the Black community in New York City continues to face challenges related to economic, educational, healthcare and social disparities. Efforts to address these challenges require a multifaceted approach, including policy changes, community engagement and investment in resources and opportunities for Black New Yorkers.

Conclusion

The spark that ignited the New York rioting was the 1863 Conscription Act, but a combustible mixture of long-festering issues—slavery, abolitionism, social class, politics, ethnicity, race, labor and capital—fueled the fire that threatened to consume the Union's largest and most important city.

In the end, we can fairly say that the New York City Draft Riots of 1863 were a crucial moment in U.S. history, reflecting the profound social and economic challenges of the time and leaving a lasting impact on the city's demographic and political landscape. Although the long-term effects of the riots are notable, improvements to the plight of New York Black people have been, to say the least, incomplete.

CHAPTER THREE
ATLANTA RACE RIOT OF 1906

The Atlanta Race Riot of 1906 was a significant and tragic event in the history of the United States, reflecting the intense racial tensions and social upheaval of the era. Following is a detailed account of the riot, its causes, events and aftermath.

Background

Racial Climate. In the early 20th century, Atlanta, Georgia, was a rapidly growing city with a sizeable Black population. However, despite economic progress and a burgeoning Black middle class, racial segregation and discrimination were deeply entrenched.

Economic Competition. The city's economic growth led to competition between Black and White workers. Black people were making strides in business and professional fields, which some White residents viewed as a threat to their economic status.

Political Tensions. The gubernatorial election of 1906 heightened racial tensions. Both candidates, Hoke Smith and Clark Howell (editors and publishers of two different major Atlanta newspapers), exploited racial fears and promoted White supremacy to gain votes.

Media Incitement. Partly owing to Smith's and Howell's influence, sensationalist and racist media reports played a critical role in stoking the violence. Newspapers, such as the Atlanta Georgian and the Atlanta News, published inflammatory stories about alleged assaults by Black men on White women. These unverified and often fabricated reports fueled public outrage—among both Black people and White people, though for different reasons.

Healthcare. Many Atlanta hospitals had segregated wards for Black patients and White patients. Segregated wards for Black patients were often underfunded and lacked essential medical resources. This resulted in inadequate staffing, limited access to medical equipment and overall inferior facilities.

Delayed or Denied Treatment. Black patients frequently experienced longer wait times and delays in receiving medical care compared to their White counterparts. In some cases, Black patients were denied access to certain medical treatments or procedures altogether.

Medical Neglect and Discrimination. Black patients faced discrimination and neglect from hospital staff, including doctors and nurses. This discriminatory treatment could manifest as dismissive attitudes, neglect of medical needs or outright refusal to provide necessary care.

Impact on Health Outcomes. Substandard care offered to Black patients in Atlanta hospitals was endemic. For Black individuals, medical care was often provided by a combination of enslaved healers, midwives and, in rare cases, White physicians who offered services to both enslaved and free Black people. However, these services were typically rudimentary and often lacked access to advanced medical treatments or facilities.

White Hospital Care. Meanwhile, hospital care available to White people in Atlanta was normally provided by trained physicians, surgeons, nurses and other healthcare professionals. Hospitals offered White people a range of medical services, including surgery, obstetrics, infectious disease treatment and general medical care.

White patients admitted to these hospitals would have received medical treatment tailored to their needs, including diagnostic evaluations, medication, surgical interventions and supportive care.

The differential in care contributed to disparities in health outcomes. Black people were more likely to experience preventable illnesses, complications from untreated conditions and higher mortality rates compared to White patients.

Jim Crow Laws. Segregated medical facilities, and segregation of Black people in general, resulted primarily due to enactment and government enforcement of Jim Crow laws. They forced racial segregation in all aspects of public life, including healthcare.

For example, at Grady Memorial Hospital (an outgrowth of the Atlanta Benevolent Home), Black patients were typically treated in separate areas of the hospital, often located in inferior facilities compared to those reserved for White patients. The hospital enforced strict segregation policies, with separate entrances, waiting rooms and hospital wards designated for Black and White patients.

The Riot

Downtown Assaults. On the evening of September 22, 1906, mobs of White men, began gathering in downtown Atlanta, converging near Five Points, the city's main intersection. Incensed by unfounded newspaper reports of Black men assaulting White women, and emboldened by rumors of a potential former-slave insurrection, the mob began attacking any Black persons they encountered, including some Black women and children, leading to widespread violence.

Streetcar Attacks. Black people traveling on streetcars were among the first targets. Mobs stopped streetcars, dragged black passengers out and beat them severely. Some were killed on the spot, while others were left gravely injured.

Night of Terror—Beatings and Lynchings. The violence quickly spread through the city. Groups of White men roamed the streets, attacking any Black people they encountered. Many Black men were beaten to death with clubs, bricks and other makeshift weapons.

Businesses Targeted. Black-owned businesses were specifically targeted. The mobs looted and set fire to these establishments, destroying livelihoods and community centers. Among the destroyed businesses were grocery stores, barber shops and cafes, which had served as important economic and social hubs for the Black community.

Home Invasions. The mob did not restrict their violence to public spaces. They invaded homes in predominantly Black neighborhoods, dragging residents out to the streets. Families were terrorized, and their properties were vandalized and set ablaze.

Massacre in Brownsville. In the Brownsville district, one of the hardest-hit areas, the violence reached a peak. The White mob's ferocity led to numerous deaths, with bodies left in the streets. Reports indicate that some victims were mutilated, and the brutality was intended to send a clear message of racial terror.

Armed Resistance. Some Black residents attempted to defend themselves. In rare instances, groups of Black men armed themselves with garden implement, bricks and anything they could find and tried to protect their homes and businesses. However, they were vastly outnumbered and outgunned, and their resistance often resulted in more severe retaliation from the mob.

Law Enforcement. The police and state militia were initially ineffective in controlling the violence. On September 24th, Georgia Governor Joseph M. Terrell declared martial law and deployed approximately 1,200 National Guard troops to attempt to restore calm. The Guard patrolled streets breaking up large groups and defending properties from destruction.

The Guard's presence proved effective, restoring order and bringing a swift end to the rioting.

The Atlanta race riot of 1906 lasted for three days, from September 22 to September 24, 1906.

Immediate Impact

Casualties. Estimates of the death toll vary, but it is generally believed that at least 25 Black people and 2 White people were killed. Many more were injured, and significant property damage occurred, particularly in Black neighborhoods such as the area known as "Sweet Auburn," which was a thriving Black community in Atlanta.

Property Damage. White rioters torched homes and businesses, and targeted community institutions, such as churches, schools, businesses, newspaper outlets and social or fraternal organizations. They shattered windows, broke down doors and vandalized property, leaving behind scenes of devastation and despair. Many Black families lost their homes and possessions from fires which ravaged entire blocks and neighborhoods necessitating family relocation, often away from Atlanta.

White rioters also looted and ransacked Black-owned stores, shops and establishments, seeking to destroy the economic livelihood of the Black community. The damage inflicted on Black neighborhoods during the 1906 Atlanta riot was profound and far-reaching, affecting the lives and livelihoods of thousands of Black residents.

Social Consequences. The riot had a devastating impact on Atlanta's Black community. It heightened racial animosity and led to increased segregation and discrimination. Many Black residents lost their homes and businesses and the sense of safety and security in the community was shattered.

Political and Social Fallout. The riot highlighted the dangers of racial demagoguery and the influence of the media in inciting violence. It also exposed the deep-rooted racial inequalities and tensions in Southern society.

Long-term Effects

The riot underscored the deep-seated racism and violence that permeated American society during the Jim Crow era and highlighted the urgent need for social and political change to address systemic inequalities and racial injustices.

Urban Development. In the aftermath of the riot, Atlanta's urban development patterns shifted, with increased segregation and the establishment of distinct Black neighborhoods. This segregation would persist for many years, influencing the city's social and economic landscape.

Civil Rights Movement. The riot was a significant precursor to the civil rights struggles that would intensify in the following decades. It underscored the need for systemic change and laid the groundwork for future activism. The NAACP (National Association for the Advancement of Colored People) was not directly formed as a result of the Atlanta Riot of 1906, but the riot was part of a broader context of racial violence and injustice that contributed to its founding.

Memory and Commemoration. The Atlanta Race Riot of 1906 remains an important historical event, commemorated by scholars, historians and civil rights activists. It serves as a reminder of the destructive power of racial hatred and the ongoing struggle for racial equality and justice in America.

Atlanta Today

The state of racism against Black people in Atlanta, GA today reflects both significant progress and ongoing challenges. Atlanta, often regarded as a hub for Black culture and business, has seen remarkable advancements in various areas, yet systemic racism and disparities still persist.

Political Representation. Atlanta has seen progress in political representation for Black individuals. The city has had Black mayors since Maynard Jackson was elected in 1973, and influential Black leaders continue to hold key positions in local government. This has led to greater advocacy for policies addressing racial inequality and Black community needs.

Economic Empowerment. Atlanta boasts a vibrant Black middle and upper class, with numerous successful Black-owned businesses and entrepreneurs. The city's economic landscape includes prominent Black business districts like Auburn Avenue and the Atlanta University Center, home to historically Black colleges and universities (HBCUs).

Cultural Influence. Atlanta is a major center for Black culture, music and arts. The city has produced influential figures in hip-hop, entertainment and media, contributing to a strong sense of cultural pride and identity among Black residents. A few recognizable names include: Ludacris, Ciara, Outkast, Tyler Perry and Gladys Knight.

Education. Institutions such as Spelman College, Morehouse College and Clark Atlanta University play pivotal roles in educating and empowering Black students. These HBCUs provide high-quality education and foster leadership within the Black community.

Economic Inequality. Despite economic progress, significant disparities persist. Black residents often face higher unemployment rates, lower wages and limited access to capital and investment opportunities compared to their White counterparts. Addressing these economic gaps requires targeted policies and investment in Black communities. In 2024, the income of Atlanta's White families significantly exceeds its Black counterpart, with median White households receiving approximately $124,048 vs median Black households receiving approximately $49,526.

Housing and Gentrification. Gentrification has led to the displacement of long-standing Black communities in Atlanta. Rising property values and rents have made it difficult for many Black families to remain in their neighborhoods, exacerbating economic and social inequalities. While it may seem that Black property sellers could simply take their profits and buy somewhere else, the reality is that suitable replacement properties available to Black people have proven difficult to identify.

Criminal Justice. Racial disparities in the criminal justice system remain a significant issue. Black individuals in Atlanta are disproportionately affected by police violence, higher arrest rates and harsher sentencing. Reforms aimed at reducing these disparities, improving community-police relations and ensuring fair treatment within the justice system are needed.

Healthcare. Health disparities are prevalent, with Black residents experiencing higher rates of chronic illnesses, lower life expectancy and limited access to quality healthcare. Addressing these disparities requires improving healthcare access, affordability and cultural competence within the medical community.

Grady Memorial Hospital. Today, Grady Memorial Hospital strives to be equally accessible to all patients, including both Black and White individuals, as well as other racial and ethnic groups. The hospital's commitment to serving all patients, regardless of background, has helped build trust within the community. However, ongoing efforts are necessary to address lingering perceptions of inequality.

<u>Education Inequality.</u> While Atlanta is home to prestigious HBCUs, public education for Black students often suffers from underfunding and disparities in resources. Efforts to improve public school funding, reduce achievement gaps and support educational attainment for Black students are essential.

Conclusion

The Atlanta Race Riot of 1906 is a testament to the deep-seated racial tensions and injustices of the time. This tragic event, fueled by economic competition, political manipulation and racial animosity, resulted in widespread violence, loss of life and profound destruction within Atlanta's Black community. The riot underscored the pervasive influence of racial prejudice and discrimination, perpetuated and amplified through sensationalist media and political exploitation.

The aftermath of the riot left lasting scars on Atlanta, reshaping its urban landscape and deepening racial segregation. The violence and devastation inflicted upon Black neighborhoods highlighted the urgent need for social and political reform to combat systemic inequalities.

Despite the progress Atlanta has made since those tumultuous days, significant challenges remain. Economic disparities, housing inequities, disparities in education, healthcare access and persistent racial injustices continue to affect Black residents disproportionately. These issues demand continued vigilance, advocacy and concerted efforts to dismantle systemic racism and promote inclusivity and equity.

CHAPTER FOUR

EAST ST. LOUIS RIOT OF 1917

The East St. Louis Riot of 1917 was one of the deadliest race riots in American history, reflecting the deep racial divide and economic disparities of the time. Following is a comprehensive overview of the causes, events and aftermath of the riot.

Background

Great Migration. The early 20th century saw the Great Migration, where large numbers of Black people moved from the rural South to the industrial North in search of better economic opportunities and to escape Jim Crow laws. East St. Louis, Illinois, became a popular destination due to its booming industrial sector.

Economic Competition. The influx of Black workers led to increased competition for jobs and housing. Many White residents and labor unions resented the new Black workers, who were often willing to work for lower wages, undermining labor strikes and threatening White workers' job security. The relatively new visible presence of Black people in the workforce and in public spaces exacerbated racial tensions. And the growing Black population led to fears among White residents of being outnumbered and economically displaced.

Labor Unrest. Labor unrest was prevalent during this period, with White labor unions often excluding Black workers. In East St. Louis, prior to the riot, there had been several recent strikes in industries like meatpacking and aluminum production, where employers used Black workers as strikebreakers, further fueling White workers' animosity.

Union Exclusion. The American Federation of Labor (AFL), one of the largest labor unions at the time, generally excluded Black workers from membership. This exclusion was based on racial prejudice and a belief that including Black workers would weaken the bargaining power of White workers.

Many craft unions, which were part of the AFL, had clauses in their constitutions that explicitly barred Black workers from joining. These unions argued that the presence of Black people in the workforce threatened White job security and wages.

Trigger Incident

CTL Union Meeting. On May 28, 1917, the Central Trades and Labor Union (CTL) held a meeting to discuss the employment of Black workers. During the meeting, White labor leaders and union members used highly inflammatory and racist rhetoric to express their frustration and anger about Black people being employed in jobs traditionally held by White workers. They rallied around the issues of Black workers undermining their strikes and driving down wages.

The charged atmosphere and incendiary language at the meeting stirred up deep-seated racial animosities. Speakers at the meeting called for action against the perceived threat posed by Black workers, implicitly or explicitly inciting the attendees to take matters into their own hands.

Initial Attacks. Initial attacks during May and June of 1917 led to minor skirmishes between the White mob and Black people. While these clashes did not immediately result in a large-scale riot, they set the stage for more severe violence by creating an atmosphere of fear and hostility.

Racial tensions continued to simmer throughout June, with White workers perpetrating sporadic incidents of violence and harassment against Black people.

On July 1, 1917, these tensions boiled over into a full-scale riot. The immediate trigger for the riot came on that day when Black residents fired upon a car carrying White men which the Black people mistakenly believed contained people who had earlier attacked a Black neighborhood. The rumor of this incident falsely held that a Black man had killed a White man, providing a pretext for White mobs to launch a large-scale attack on the Black community.

The Riot

On July 1, a massive mob of White residents (mostly men), estimated to number in the thousands, rampaged through Black neighborhoods in East St. Louis. They set fire to homes and businesses, looted properties and brutally attacked any Black individuals they encountered.

Casualties. Violence to persons was extreme and indiscriminate. The White crowd lynched, beat and shot Black people. Many were forced to flee their homes to escape the mob, leading to significant displacement and loss of property.

The next day, July 2, White mobs, some of whom were reportedly organized and armed, began a systematic attack on Black neighborhoods in East St. Louis. They again set fire to homes and businesses, and shot, beat and lynched Black residents attempting to flee the violence. It is difficult to over-emphasize the extent of the brutality involved in these incidents.

National Guard Activated. Also on July 2nd, in response to the rapidly escalating violence and chaos, Illinois Governor Frank O. Lowden made the decision to deploy 1,500 National Guard troops to East St. Louis.

Even with support from the National Guard, local police were largely ineffective in stopping the violence. And in some cases, law enforcement officers were accused of participating in or abetting the attacks.

Federal Troops Deployed. Finally, on July 3rd, President Woodrow Wilson deployed 1,000 U.S Army troops to the city. The troops patrolled the streets, enforced curfews and worked to separate warring factions. Their presence helped to deter further violence and bring the situation under control. Additionally, their authority and discipline helped to reassure the community and restore a sense of safety and security.

Immediate Impact

Casualties. Estimates of the death toll vary, with reports suggesting that between 39 and 150 Black people were killed. Hundreds more were injured. The official death toll for White people was logged as seven.

The violence displaced thousands of Black families, many fleeing across the Mississippi River to St. Louis, Missouri. The riot left a lasting scar on the Black community, both physically and psychologically.

Racial Segregation Deepens. The riots deepened and solidified racial segregation in East St. Louis, with Black people increasingly confined to specific neighborhoods. The violence and fear generated by the riots fostered long-lasting distrust between Black and White communities and between Black people and the police.

<u>Influence on Civil Rights Movements.</u> The brutality of the riots highlighted the urgent need for civil rights advocacy. Organizations like the NAACP (organized in 1909) used the events in East St. Louis to galvanize support for anti-lynching legislation and other civil rights initiatives.

<u>National Awareness.</u> The riots brought national attention to the extent of racial animosity in American society. Reports and photographs of the violence shocked the nation, leading to widespread condemnation and calls for racial justice and equality. Prominent figures such as W.E.B. Du Bois and the NAACP highlighted the atrocity, calling for federal intervention and greater protections for Black people. The NAACP organized a Silent Parade in New York City on July 28, 1917, to protest the violence and racial injustice.

<u>Public Perception and Media Coverage.</u> Media coverage of the riots often reflected and reinforced racial biases. Despite the facts, some newspapers depicted Black people as instigators of the violence, perpetuating stereotypes and justifying the actions of the White mobs.

Long-term Effects

<u>Civil Rights Advocacy.</u> The East St. Louis Riot galvanized the civil rights movement, leading to increased activism and efforts to address racial violence and inequality. It underscored the need for federal anti-lynching legislation and improved government enforcement of civil rights protections.

<u>Urban Segregation.</u> The riot contributed to the entrenchment of racial segregation in East St. Louis and other Northern cities. Black people were often forced into segregated neighborhoods and faced ongoing discrimination in housing and employment.

<u>Historical Memory.</u> The East St. Louis Riot is commemorated and studied as part of the broader struggle for civil rights and racial equality in the United States.

East St. Louis Today

Systemic racism continues to significantly affect East St. Louis today, manifesting in various forms, particularly environmental and economic injustices. The city, whose population is approximately 98 percent Black, faces severe challenges including environmental degradation and lack of access to adequate healthcare and services.

<u>Environmental Racism.</u> Environmental racism is a major concern, with toxic waste and pollution disproportionately affecting Black residents. Activist groups like Empire 13 are working to address these issues through community cleanups and raising awareness. Their efforts highlight the dire conditions in the area, such as the pervasive presence of trash and debris, and aim to spark legislative changes to combat these injustices.

<u>Economic Challenges.</u> The economic disparities are also stark. Despite featuring an overwhelmingly Black populace, median White household income substantially outpaces its Black counterpart, with White families receiving approximately $70,8831 while Black households receive around $27,3011.

East St. Louis is also one of the most distressed small cities in the United States, a situation exacerbated by decades of systemic racism that have led to disinvestment and neglect. Efforts are ongoing to secure federal assistance and implement regular maintenance and cleanup operations to improve the living conditions for its residents.

Conclusion

The East St. Louis Riot of 1917 stands as a tragic and pivotal moment in American history, illustrating the profound racial tensions and systemic injustices that plagued the nation during the early 20th century. This harrowing event, one of the deadliest race riots in U.S. history, was fueled by economic competition, labor strife and deeply ingrained racial animosities. The riot not only resulted in substantial loss of life and property but also left enduring scars on the community, exacerbating racial segregation and distrust between Black and White residents.

The immediate aftermath of the riot saw the displacement of thousands of Black families and highlighted the vulnerability of Black communities in the face of unchecked racial violence. The deployment of state and federal troops, while necessary to quell the violence, underscored the failure of local law enforcement to protect Black citizens from mob attacks. This failure further deepened the mistrust and resentment felt by the Black community towards law enforcement authorities.

The East St. Louis Riot reverberated across the nation, drawing attention to pervasive racial injustices and prompting renewed calls for civil rights protections and anti-lynching legislation. The riot became a rallying cry for civil rights activists and organizations like the NAACP, galvanizing their efforts to combat racial violence and discrimination.

In the decades since the riot, East St. Louis has struggled with persistent challenges stemming from systemic racism, including environmental degradation, economic disparities and inadequate access to essential services. These ongoing issues underscore the enduring legacy of racial inequality and the urgent need for comprehensive social and economic reforms.

The East St. Louis Riot of 1917 serves as a somber reminder of the ongoing struggle for racial justice and equality in America. The lessons learned from this tragic event continue to resonate today, urging us to confront and dismantle systemic racism in all its forms and to strive towards a future where every individual is treated with dignity, fairness and justice. Only through concerted efforts to address these historical injustices can we hope to build a more inclusive and equitable society for future generations.

CHAPTER FIVE

THE CHICAGO RACE RIOT OF 1919

The Chicago Race Riot of 1919 was one of the most violent and significant race riots in American history, occurring during a period of heightened racial tensions known as the "Red Summer." Following is a comprehensive overview of the causes, events and aftermath of the riot.

Background

Great Migration. Similar to the East St. Louis Riot, the Chicago Race Riot was partly fueled by the Great Migration, where Black families moved from the South to the North in large numbers to find work and to escape violence and the restrictions of Jim Crow laws. Chicago's Black population grew significantly during this time period, leading to the, by now, familiar refrain of increased competition for jobs and housing.

Economic Competition. Many Black people found employment in Chicago's burgeoning industrial sector. Factories, stockyards, steel mills and railroads provided numerous job opportunities, though these were often the least desirable positions and characterized by low pay, harsh or dangerous working conditions and limited opportunities for advancement.

Working Conditions. Despite finding employment, Black people faced deeply entrenched racial discrimination once on the job. They were often the last hired and first fired and were generally paid less than their White counterparts for the same work. Segregation in the workplace was common.

Stockyards and Steel. Many Black people were employed in the Union Stockyards, where they performed physically demanding and dangerous tasks such as slaughtering animals, processing meat and handling hides. Others worked in steel mills, often in the most difficult and hazardous positions, such as furnace operators, loaders and laborers. Jobs for Black people in the railroad industry included track maintenance, porters, brakemen and freight handlers.

Pullman Porters. Pullman porters were a rare exception to the "undesirable or hazardous" standard. Pullman porters worked for the Pullman Company, which operated sleeper cars on trains. Their primary duties included attending to passengers' needs, handling luggage, setting up sleeping berths and maintaining the cleanliness of the train cars. Porters were required to maintain a polished appearance and conduct themselves with utmost professionalism, embodying the company's emphasis on luxury and refinement.

Becoming a Pullman porter provided one of the few relatively stable and well-paying job opportunities available. While the work was demanding, it offered a steady income, which was critical for supporting Black families and communities. Although base wages were low, porters could earn additional income through tips from passengers, which could significantly supplement their earnings.

Pullman porters were also seen as leaders within the Black community. Their travels exposed them to different parts of the country and to various socio-economic conditions, broadening their perspectives. This experience often translated into leadership roles in civil rights movements and community organizations.

Service Jobs. Many Black women were employed as maids, cooks and laundresses in private homes. While both men and women worked as janitors, cleaners and maintenance workers in office buildings, hotels and public facilities.

Visibility of Black people. The breadth and variety of jobs undertaken by Black people—especially uniformed Black people—meant that they were highly visible in the workforce, which led to greater resentment among White workers. Economic competition between Black people and White people was increasing and became a significant source of tension between the Races.

Trigger Incident

In 1919, the beaches and swimming areas in Chicago were routinely segregated, often informally, with one area open to White people only and another for Black people. On July 27, 1919, a Black teenager named Eugene Williams and several of his friends were using a makeshift raft to swim and float in Lake Michigan. This raft drifted into an area of the water that was informally designated for White beachgoers.

When the raft crossed into the "White" section of the water, a group of White men on the shore began throwing stones at Eugene and his friends, allegedly in an attempt to drive them back. One of the stones struck Eugene Williams on the head.

After being hit, Eugene Williams lost consciousness and subsequently drowned. His body was later recovered from the lake. The Black community demanded the arrest of the White man who threw the rock. However, the police refused to arrest the suspect and instead arrested a Black man, which further inflamed tensions and sparked outrage among the Black community.

The presence of the raft in "prohibited" waters, the stoning by the White beachgoers and the subsequent refusal by Police to make an arrest were crucial elements in the chain of events that led to the subsequent outbreak of mass violence.

The Riot

Initial Violence. Clashes between Black and White residents erupted almost immediately after the incident. More organized rioting began on the South Side of Chicago and quickly spread, with White mobs attacking Black neighborhoods and Black individuals and groups defending themselves and their communities. As the violence continued, both sides engaged in attacks on individuals and property.

The rioting continued through the following day, with widespread violence affecting various parts of the city. White mobs attacked Black neighborhoods, looting and burning homes and businesses. Black people fought back, resulting in street battles and further casualties.

Black people organized to protect their neighborhoods and themselves from White mobs, arming themselves with weapons like bricks, stones and firearms. They set up barricades and patrols to defend against attacks on their homes and businesses.

Black Retaliation. In some instances, Black groups actively retaliated against White aggressors. This included confronting and attacking White individuals who were participating in the violence or were seen as threats. And Black groups actively targeted areas of the city where White rioters were gathering, attempting to push them back and prevent further incursions into Black neighborhoods.

Police Response. Having initially declined to make an arrest at the beach following Williams' death, subsequent police response was criticized as tepid. As the violence escalated, Black residents reported a lack of police protection and intervention. Many Black people felt abandoned by the police and left to fend for themselves against White mobs that were attacking their homes and businesses.

The police response drew criticism for its alleged bias and discrimination against Black people. There were reports of police officers siding with White rioters and participating in the racial violence. Black residents later reported feeling that the police were not impartial enforcers of the law but were instead complicit in perpetuating racial injustice and inequality.

In any case, the police were unable to effectively control the violence and prevent further escalation. Law enforcement agencies were overwhelmed by the scale of the unrest and lacked the resources and training to handle the situation effectively.

National Guard Deployed. As the riot escalated and the violence spread throughout the city, it became clear that local law enforcement agencies were overwhelmed, and that additional support was needed to restore order. Accordingly, on July 29th, the second day of the Riot, Illinois Governor, Frank Lowden deployed approximately 6,000 National Guard troops to Chicago to assist in quelling the unrest and protecting the public safety.

Troops were deployed to patrol the streets, enforce curfews and establish barriers to separate warring groups. Their presence helped to stabilize the situation, but significant rioting continued until August 3rd—a total of seven days. By that point, physical exhaustion combined with the Guard presence and calls by community and religious leaders for calm resulted in a gradual decrease in the violence.

Finally, on August 3rd, a collection of state and local government officials declared the violence to be at an end, though tensions remained high in the aftermath of the riot.

Immediate Impacts

Casualties. The Chicago Race Riot of 1919 resulted in 38 deaths. Among those killed, 23 were Black and 15 were White. The riot also left over 500 people injured.

Property Damage. The total dollar amount of property damage done during the Chicago Race Riot of 1919 was estimated at around $250,000 (approximately $700,000 in today's dollars). Over 1,000 Black families were left homeless, their homes destroyed by arson.

Black Churches Targeted. Black churches and community centers, central to the social and cultural life of the community, were targeted for destruction. One such institution was Quinn Chapel African Methodist Episcopal Church, one of the oldest Black churches in Chicago. Other Black churches in the area suffered similar fates.

Public Property. Public infrastructure such as streetcars, streetlights and public buildings, mainly in Black areas, were also damaged or destroyed during the riot. Streetcars were overturned and set ablaze in the streets; public buildings, including schools and government offices, were vandalized.

The immediate consequence of the riot included the deepening of racial divisions in Chicago. Black people became more resolute in their demands for civil rights and equal treatment, while many White residents became more entrenched in their opposition to integration in the workplace and in society in general.

Long-term Effects

The Chicago Race Riot of 1919 was a pivotal moment in the early civil rights movement. It underscored the urgent need for addressing racial inequalities and preventing racial violence. The NAACP and other organizations used the riot to continue their push for federal anti-lynching legislation and greater civil rights protections.

But the riot also led to increased segregation in Chicago, forcing Black people to remain in overcrowded and impoverished neighborhoods, and to face ongoing discrimination in housing and employment.

Chicago Today

Following are some key aspects of the state of racism in Chicago today:

Systemic Racism. Systemic racism continues to be a significant issue in Chicago, affecting various aspects of life for its residents, particularly Black and Brown communities.

Housing Segregation and Disparities. Chicago remains highly segregated, with neighborhoods predominantly Black or Latino often experiencing disinvestment, lack of resources and poorer living conditions compared to predominantly White neighborhoods. Historical redlining practices and discriminatory lending practices have contributed to these disparities, limiting access to quality housing and perpetuating economic inequalities.

Education Inequities. Public schools in predominantly Black and Latino neighborhoods tend to have fewer resources, higher teacher turnover rates and lower academic outcomes compared to schools in predominantly White neighborhoods.

Police Brutality and Criminal Justice. The Chicago Police Department (CPD) has a long history of misconduct and systemic issues, including racial profiling, excessive use of force against Black and Brown residents and lack of accountability for officers involved in misconduct. Incidents like the Laquan McDonald shooting in 2014 and subsequent protests highlight deep-seated issues of police brutality and racial bias.

Economic Disparities. Black communities in Chicago face higher unemployment rates, lower median incomes and fewer opportunities for economic mobility compared to White residents. Discriminatory practices in hiring, promotions and access to business loans contribute to these disparities, perpetuating a cycle of economic disadvantage.

Income disparities between Black and White Chicagoans also remain prominent today. In 2024, the median White household received an income of $99,363 per year while their Black counterparts received income of only $40,184.

Healthcare Disparities. Access to healthcare services and health outcomes continue to vary significantly based on race and socioeconomic status in Chicago. Black communities often have limited access to quality healthcare facilities, leading to higher rates of chronic diseases, infant mortality and shorter life expectancy compared to White residents.

Environmental Justice. Environmental racism is evident in Chicago, where predominantly Black and Latino neighborhoods bear a disproportionate burden of environmental hazards such as pollution, industrial waste and lack of green spaces. These environmental injustices contribute to higher rates of respiratory illnesses and other health problems in these communities.

Political Representation and Advocacy. Despite being a city with a significant Black population (45.33% are White, 29.22% are Black), political representation and decision-making processes do not adequately reflect the needs and interests of Black communities. This lack of representation hinders efforts to address systemic racism effectively through policy and legislative reforms.

Community Efforts. Efforts to address systemic racism in Chicago are ongoing and involve grassroots activism, community organizing, advocacy by civil rights organizations and policy initiatives at local, state and federal levels. While progress has been made in some areas, the persistence of systemic racism underscores the need for sustained commitment to equity, justice and inclusive policies to create a more equitable Chicago for all its residents.

Conclusion

The Chicago Race Riot of 1919 reminds us of the deep-seated racial tensions and systemic injustices that have plagued the city for generations. Sparked by the tragic death of Eugene Williams and fueled by longstanding racial discrimination and economic disparities, the riot unleashed a wave of violence and destruction that left an indelible mark on Chicago's history.

This chapter has provided a comprehensive exploration of the causes, events and aftermath of the riot, highlighting its profound impact on the trajectory of race relations and civil rights in America. The riot underscored the urgent need to confront racial inequalities and systemic racism, both in Chicago and across the nation.

In the aftermath of the riot, the city saw a surge in activism and calls for justice from the Black community, demanding an end to discriminatory practices and greater civil rights protections. Organizations like the NAACP used the riot as a rallying cry to continue its push for federal anti-lynching legislation and other reforms aimed at addressing racial injustice.

However, despite some progress over the decades, systemic racism continues to cast a long shadow over Chicago today. From housing segregation and economic disparities to unequal access to education and healthcare, Black communities still face substantial barriers to equality and opportunity. The legacy of the riot persists in the form of entrenched inequalities that perpetuate cycles of poverty and marginalization.

Efforts to dismantle systemic racism in Chicago are ongoing, driven by grassroots activism, advocacy and policy initiatives aimed at achieving racial equity and justice. Yet, the road ahead remains challenging, requiring sustained commitment and collective action to create a city where all residents can thrive regardless of race or background.

The Chicago Race Riot of 1919 entreats us to continue the fight for racial justice and to confront systemic racism in all its forms. As we reflect on this dark chapter in Chicago's history, we must also look forward with resolve, working towards a future where equity, inclusion and justice are not just aspirations but realities for every Chicagoan.

CHAPTER SIX

THE TULSA RACE MASSACRE OF 1921

The Tulsa Race Massacre of 1921, also known as the Tulsa Race Riot, is one of the most horrific episodes of racial violence in American history. It took place in the affluent Black community of Greenwood in Tulsa, Oklahoma. Following is a comprehensive overview of the events, causes and aftermath of the massacre.

Background

In 1920, Greenwood, OK was one of the wealthiest Black communities in the United States. An estimated 75% to 80% of residents were Black. The community earned the nickname "Black Wall Street" due to its economic success and the wealth generated by its residents.

Establishment. The Greenwood District was established in the early 1900s, primarily by Black settlers who moved to Tulsa seeking opportunities in the oil industry and other professions. Despite facing racial segregation and discrimination, the Greenwood District thrived economically and became a bustling hub of Black entrepreneurship and featuring a vibrant cultural scene.

The district boasted an impressive array of Black-owned businesses, which contributed to its reputation as a prosperous and self-sufficient community. Among them was a wide range of establishments, including grocery stores, banks, hotels, theaters, restaurants, insurance brokerages and more.

Wealth Accumulation. The economic prosperity of Black Wall Street allowed many residents to accumulate wealth and achieve financial success. Homeownership was common, and property values in the district were relatively high.

Cultural Significance. Beyond its economic achievements, Black Wall Street was a center of Black culture and community life. It was home to churches, schools, social clubs and other institutions that fostered a strong sense of identity and belonging among residents.

Educational Opportunities. The Greenwood District's dedication to education and the advancement of Black youth was a cornerstone of its success and prosperity. The community supported a number of schools and educational programs that provided opportunities for academic and personal growth. Among those opportunities were the following:

Booker T. Washington High School. Established in 1913 and named after the prominent African American educator and leader, Booker T. Washington High School was one of the most important educational institutions in Greenwood. It provided high-quality education to Black students during a time when segregation limited their access to educational resources. The school emphasized academic excellence and vocational training, preparing students for both higher education and skilled trades.

The school gained a reputation for its rigorous academic standards and the success of its graduates, many of whom went on to attend colleges and universities or start successful careers.

Masonic Lodge Educational Programs. The Masonic Lodge in Greenwood was not just a fraternal organization but also played a significant role in promoting education. The lodge organized scholarships, tutoring programs and educational workshops for young people in the community. These programs helped to ensure that Black youth had access to educational opportunities beyond the classroom, fostering a culture of lifelong learning and academic achievement.

YWCA and YMCA. Both the Young Women's Christian Association (YWCA) and the Young Men's Christian Association (YMCA) had branches in Greenwood that offered a variety of educational and recreational programs for youth. These organizations provided after-school programs, literacy classes and leadership training, helping to develop well-rounded individuals prepared for future challenges.

Business and Professional Education. Greenwood was home to several business colleges and vocational schools that provided specialized training in fields such as accounting, typing and other office skills. These institutions were crucial for the economic success of Black Wall Street, as they prepared individuals for roles in the many businesses that thrived in the district.

Professional Development. In addition to formal schooling, many business owners and professionals in Greenwood mentored young people, offering apprenticeships and on-the-job training that provided practical experience and skill development.

Community Support for Education. The residents of Greenwood placed a high value on education, understanding its importance for personal and community advancement. Parents, community leaders and business owners actively supported educational initiatives, often funding scholarships and school programs.

Engagement. Community events frequently included educational components, such as public lectures, debates and cultural programs, which enriched the intellectual life of Greenwood's residents.

Libraries and Reading Rooms. Greenwood had several libraries and reading rooms that were accessible to the public. These facilities provided important resources for students and adults alike, offering access to books, newspapers and other educational materials.

Despite the tragic destruction of Greenwood during the Tulsa Race Massacre of 1921, the legacy of its commitment to education and community upliftment continues to inspire generations.

Trigger Incident

On May 30, 1921, Dick Rowland, a 19-year-old Black shoeshiner, entered an elevator in the Drexel Building operated by a White woman, Sarah Page. What happened next is not fully documented, but it is believed that Rowland either stepped on Page's foot or stumbled into her, causing her to scream. A clerk in a nearby store heard the scream and assumed that an assault had taken place, subsequently contacting the police.

When questioned, Sarah Page reportedly told the police that Rowland had grabbed her arm, but she did not press charges or claim that he had assaulted her in a more severe manner. Despite Page's description of the encounter, local press sensationalized the incident, with the Tulsa Tribune running an incendiary article that heightened racial tensions.

The exact title of the article is often cited as "Nab Negro for Attacking Girl in an Elevator." This article, combined with an accompanying editorial titled "To Lynch Negro Tonight," played a significant role in inciting outrage among the White population.

The ambiguity and lack of definitive statements from Sarah Page herself have led historians to rely on available police records, newspaper accounts and testimonies from that time, many of which are biased or incomplete. This incident, however, is generally accepted as the spark that led to the catastrophic events of the Tulsa Race Massacre.

The Massacre

Initial Confrontation. On the evening of May 31, a White mob gathered outside the courthouse where Rowland was held, demanding his lynching. In response, a group of armed Black men, many of whom were World War I veterans, went to the courthouse to protect Rowland and prevent a lynching. A confrontation ensued and shots were fired.

Escalation. The situation rapidly escalated into a full-scale riot. White mobs, some deputized and armed by local authorities, attacked the Greenwood District. White rioters looted, burned and destroyed homes, businesses and churches in Greenwood. The attackers used guns, bombs and even privately-owned planes to drop incendiary devices, leading to widespread destruction.

Use of Airplanes. It is notable that the Tulsa Massacre marked the only documented use of airplanes during a riot in America. The use of planes highlighted several critical and disturbing aspects of the event:

Scale and Organization of the Attack. The involvement of planes demonstrated a high level of premeditation, coordination and organization among the White attackers. This was not a spontaneous outbreak of violence but a calculated assault using advanced means.

Escalation of Violence. The use of airplanes to drop incendiary devices and fire upon the Black residents of Greenwood marked a significant escalation in the methods of violence historically employed by White rioters. It transformed the massacre from a ground-based riot into a more deadly and far-reaching attack, showcasing an alarming willingness to use military-style tactics against civilians.

Systematic Destruction. The aerial attacks facilitated the systematic and widespread destruction of the Greenwood District. By setting fires from the air, the attackers ensured that the devastation was comprehensive, contributing to the near-total destruction of homes, businesses and infrastructure.

Impunity and Lack of Accountability. The fact that private planes could be used in such an attack without criminal repercussions indicates a significant level of impunity for the perpetrators. It reflects the deep-seated racial animosity and the lack of legal consequences for perpetrators of the massacre.

Technological Advantage. The use of aircraft also underscores the technological disparity, power imbalance and the vulnerability of the Black community in the face of such advanced means of attack.

National Guard Mobilization. In the early hours of June 1, 1921, the second day of the massacre, as the violence continued to intensify and spread, local officials, realizing they could not manage the situation, requested assistance from the state government.

That morning, Oklahoma Governor Robertson declared martial law and mobilized approximately 1,500 National Guard troops to assist local authorities in managing the riot. National Guard units began arriving in Tulsa to restore order later that day.

Internment of Black Residents. As part of the effort to control the situation, thousands of Black residents of Greenwood were rounded up and detained by local authorities and National Guard troops. This was ostensibly for their protection, but it also served to contain and control the Black population.

Detention Centers. Authorities transported Black residents to various makeshift detention centers around the city. These included: The Convention Hall (later known as the Tulsa Municipal Building); McNulty Park (a baseball stadium); and various churches and schools.

The conditions in these detention centers were harsh. Detainees were held in overcrowded and unsanitary conditions, with inadequate access to food, water and medical care. Families were often separated, adding to the trauma and chaos.

Identification Process. Black detainees were required to wear identification tags or arm bands, issued by the authorities, to indicate that they had been processed and were allowed to move about. White employers or White residents had to vouch for Black detainees to secure their release.

Psychological Effects of Internment. The massacre itself was a horrifying experience, with many Black residents witnessing the destruction of their homes, businesses and neighborhoods, as well as the brutal killing of friends and family members. Their internment only intensified this their sense of helplessness, fear and terror.

Immediate Impact

Casualties. Estimates of the death toll vary, but it is believed that between 100 and 300 Black people were killed. Many more were injured, and thousands were left homeless. Deaths of between 10 and 20 White people were also reported.

Property Damage. The massacre resulted in the complete destruction of the Greenwood District. Approximately 35 city blocks were burned to the ground, including over 1,200 homes, businesses, schools and churches. The economic impact was devastating, with property damage estimated at around $1.5 million in 1921 dollars (over $25 million today).

Displacement. Thousands of Black residents of Greenwood were left homeless. Some survivors were forced into internment camps, and many Black people fled Tulsa, never to return. Those that remained sought refuge in makeshift tent camps provided by the Red Cross, community churches or with relatives and friends outside the affected area.

Financial Devastation. The destruction of homes, businesses and personal property led to financial devastation of the community. Many Black residents lost their life savings and the economic heart of the Black community was destroyed.

To add to the utter financial ruin, insurance companies denied claims for the property damage, as most policies had riot exclusion clauses.

Emotional and Psychological Effects. In addition to the economic and financial losses, survivors of the massacre experienced deep psychological trauma, including grief, fear and intractable anxiety. Many children and adults witnessed horrific acts of violence, leading to long-term mental health issues.

Disruption of Community Life. The social fabric of the Greenwood community lay utterly decimated. Churches, schools and social organizations had been destroyed and a number of vital community leaders were killed or displaced; not to mention the significant disruption in education and social services for Black people in Greenwood.

Long-term Consequences

Loss of Collateral and Credit. The destruction of businesses and homes meant that many Black residents lost their collateral and creditworthiness, making it difficult to secure loans and investment to rebuild. Systemic racism in banking and finance further restricted access to capital for the Black community.

There was an opportunity for governments to step in and help the community, but local and state governments provided little to no financial assistance for rebuilding. In fact, city leaders quickly moved to rezone the area to prevent the Black community from rebuilding, although these plans were eventually abandoned.

Reduced Economic Opportunities. Of course, the massacre resulted in long-term economic decline in Greenwood. The vibrant economy of Black Wall Street has never fully recovered. The community's economic base was substantially decimated, leading to reduced employment opportunities and lower overall economic activity there.

The loss of wealth and property had intergenerational impacts, contributing to the ongoing wealth gap between Black and White families in Tulsa and beyond. The inability to pass down assets and businesses to future generations deprived descendants of the economic opportunities that come from generational wealth.

Marginalization and Economic Inequality. In the decades following the Tulsa Race Massacre, a variety of city economic policies and practices continued to disadvantage the Black community in Tulsa, limiting opportunities for economic advancement. Examples of such policies include:

Urban Renewal Projects. Throughout the mid-20th century, Tulsa, like many other American cities, embarked on urban renewal projects that disproportionately targeted Black neighborhoods for demolition. These projects resulted in the destruction of many remaining Black-owned businesses and homes in the Greenwood District.

Highway Routing. Additionally, the construction of highways and other infrastructure projects frequently cut through Black neighborhoods, further displacing residents and disrupting community cohesion.

Zoning Laws. Zoning laws were also used to segregate Black residents into specific areas, limiting their access to better housing and business locations. Immediately following the Tulsa Race Massacre, city officials proposed to rezone the destroyed Greenwood District from residential to industrial to prevent Black residents from rebuilding. These laws restricted the ability of the Black community to rebuild and expand their economic base.

Psychological Trauma and Economic Productivity. The psychological trauma Greenwood residents suffered resulting from the Tulsa Race Massacre had profound and long-lasting effects on both individuals and the community as a whole. Such effects are more difficult to quantify. But understanding them is important to appreciate the experience the Black community suffered from the Massacre.

Mental Health Impact. Greenwood survivors almost certainly experienced a range of mental health issues such as post-traumatic stress disorder (PTSD), depression, anxiety and survivor's guilt. These conditions interfered with their ability to function effectively in daily life, including their capacity to work and engage in economic activities.

Psychological trauma can also manifest in physical health problems such as chronic pain, cardiovascular issues and autoimmune disorders. These health challenges almost certainly limited some survivors' ability to work or at a minimum, led to increased healthcare costs, further straining the community's economic well-being.

Interpersonal Relationships. Trauma also affects relationships with family, friends and the broader community. Difficulty in forming and maintaining supportive relationships can contribute to feelings of isolation and despair and exacerbate other mental health issues, potentially impacting job performance and economic stability.

Educational and Career Trajectories. Children and descendants of survivors may have been indirectly affected by intergenerational trauma, which can manifest in academic struggles, low self-esteem and challenges in building successful careers. These factors can hinder economic prospects and perpetuate cycles of poverty and disadvantage for multiple generations.

Economic Opportunities. Survivors' psychological trauma most likely limited survivors' ability to pursue education, training or career advancement opportunities. It probably also resulted in job loss, absenteeism and underemployment due to difficulties in coping with workplace stress or triggers related to the Massacre.

Investment in Recovery. Individuals and communities impacted by trauma often require significant resources and support to address their mental health needs and rebuild their lives. Financial resources that could have been invested in education, entrepreneurship or economic development may instead have been directed toward trauma recovery efforts.

Erosion of Social Networks. The destruction of Greenwood disrupted the social and economic networks that were crucial for business and community support, making collective economic recovery even more difficult.

Lack of Justice. The perpetrators of the massacre were never held accountable. No one was prosecuted or punished for the violence and local government and law enforcement failed to provide justice for the victims.

Ignored by History. To add insult to injury, historical accounts largely ignored the Massacre effectively suppressing the topic for many decades and hiding it from the eyes of well-meaning White people throughout the country.

Historical Recognition. In recent years, there has been a growing recognition of the Tulsa Race Massacre. Scholars, activists and descendants of survivors have worked to uncover and document the events. Memorials and educational programs have been established to honor the victims and educate the public.

Also relatively recently, the Massacre has been the subject of books, documentaries and other forms of media, bringing greater awareness to this dark chapter in American history. These serve as reminders of the consequences of racial hatred and the importance of addressing systemic racism.

Tulsa Today

In contemporary Tulsa, racial dynamics continue to be complex and are influenced by historical legacies, socioeconomic disparities and ongoing efforts toward reconciliation and progress. Following you will find some key aspects of the racial situation in Tulsa today.

Racial Composition. Tulsa is a diverse city with a population that includes a mix of racial and ethnic backgrounds. According to recent census data, the city's population is predominantly White, with Black people amounting to about 15% of total residents.

Segregation Patterns. While Tulsa is not officially or legally segregated, residential patterns often reflect historic divisions along racial lines. There are neighborhoods with predominantly Black, White, Hispanic/Latino and Native American populations, which contribute to disparities in access to resources and opportunities.

Income Inequality. Like many cities in the United States, Tulsa experiences significant income inequality along racial lines. In 2024, the median White household received about $61,825, while median Black household income was reported as $39,779.

Education. Disparities in educational attainment persist, with students from minority backgrounds often facing challenges such as underfunded schools, lack of access to quality educational resources and disproportionate disciplinary actions. Efforts to address these disparities include initiatives focused on equity in education and expanding access to early childhood education programs.

Tulsa Race Massacre Legacy. The Tulsa Race Massacre of 1921 continues to loom large in the city's collective memory. Efforts to acknowledge and reckon with this history have gained momentum in recent years, including initiatives to commemorate the victims, educate the public and promote racial healing and reconciliation.

Greenwood District. The Greenwood District has experienced efforts at revitalization in recent years, including economic development initiatives and investments aimed at preserving its historic significance while fostering economic opportunities for the Black community. Some examples include:

Greenwood Rising History Center. Opened in 2021, Greenwood Rising is a state-of-the-art history center that commemorates the 1921 Tulsa Race Massacre and celebrates the resilience of the Greenwood community. It serves as an educational and cultural hub, attracting visitors and fostering a deeper understanding of the district's history. The center plays a crucial role in preserving the legacy of Black Wall Street while promoting tourism and economic activity in the area.

Black Wall Street Chamber of Commerce. Established in 2018, the Black Wall Street Chamber of Commerce supports the economic development of Black-owned businesses in Tulsa. It provides resources, networking opportunities and advocacy for entrepreneurs and business owners in the Greenwood District. The chamber offers business workshops, mentorship programs, and access to capital, helping to foster a thriving business environment in the historic district.

Greenwood Cultural Center. Established in 1995, the Greenwood Cultural Center serves as a community gathering space and a venue for cultural events, educational programs and social services. It aims to preserve the heritage of Greenwood and promote cultural awareness. The center hosts exhibits, performances and workshops that celebrate African American culture and history, contributing to the district's cultural and economic revitalization.

Greenwood Main Street Program. Established in 2010, the Main Street program focuses on revitalizing the commercial corridor of Greenwood through beautification projects, infrastructure improvements and business support services. Efforts include streetscaping, building facade improvements and the development of public spaces to create an attractive and vibrant environment for businesses and visitors.

North Tulsa Economic Development Initiative (NTEDI). Established in 2007, NTEDI is dedicated to fostering economic growth and improving the quality of life in North Tulsa, including the Greenwood District. It focuses on attracting investment, supporting local businesses and enhancing infrastructure. NTEDI has been involved in various projects, such as affordable housing developments, commercial property renovations, and the creation of job opportunities for residents.

Greenwood District Master Plan. Developed in 2018, the master plan was developed with input from various stakeholders, including community leaders, local residents, business owners and city officials, to address the unique needs and opportunities of the Greenwood area. The master plan outlines a comprehensive vision for the preservation and revitalization of the Greenwood District, balancing historical preservation with modern economic development. The plan includes guidelines for maintaining the architectural integrity of historic buildings, promoting heritage tourism, and encouraging new development that respects the district's historical significance.

Preservation of Historic Landmarks. Efforts have been made to preserve and restore key historic landmarks in Greenwood, such as the Vernon AME Church and the Mabel B. Little Heritage House. These sites serve as reminders of the district's rich history and as focal points for community activities.

Education and Awareness Programs. Programs aimed at educating the public about the history and significance of the Greenwood District have been implemented. These include school curricula, public lectures and community workshops.

Annual Events and Festivals. Events such as the Juneteenth Celebration and the Tulsa Race Massacre Centennial Commemoration attract visitors and highlight the cultural and historical significance of Greenwood. These events not only honor the legacy of the district but also stimulate economic activity by bringing together local vendors, artists and entrepreneurs.

Civil Rights and Social Justice Organizations. Tulsa is home to various civil rights and social justice organizations that advocate for racial equity, police reform, criminal justice reform and other issues impacting marginalized communities. At this writing, such organizations include:

Black Lives Matter Tulsa. Black Lives Matter (BLM) Tulsa is a local chapter of the national movement advocating against systemic racism and police brutality. They organize protests, community events and educational initiatives to raise awareness and demand justice for Black lives.

Tulsa Dream Center. The Tulsa Dream Center provides programs and services to address poverty, homelessness and food insecurity in underserved communities. They offer educational resources, job training and support services to empower individuals and families to break the cycle of poverty.

NAACP Tulsa Branch. The NAACP Tulsa Branch advocates for civil rights, social justice and racial equality. They focus on issues such as voting rights, criminal justice reform and economic empowerment for Black communities.

Community Service Council of Greater Tulsa. The Community Service Council (CSC) of Greater Tulsa is a nonprofit organization that works to address social and economic disparities in the community. They conduct research, provide data analysis and collaborate with local agencies to develop policies and programs that promote equity and improve quality of life.

Tulsa Justice Advocates. Tulsa Justice Advocates is a grassroots organization dedicated to fighting for racial and social justice in Tulsa. They advocate for police accountability, criminal justice reform and community-led solutions to address systemic inequality and injustice.

John Hope Franklin Center for Reconciliation. The John Hope Franklin Center for Reconciliation promotes understanding, healing and reconciliation in Tulsa and beyond. They organize educational programs, community dialogues and cultural events to confront the city's history of racial violence and work towards a more equitable future.

Tulsa African Ancestral Society. The Tulsa African Ancestral Society (TAAS) is dedicated to preserving and celebrating African heritage and culture in Tulsa. They provide educational resources, cultural events and community outreach programs to empower individuals and promote racial pride and identity.

The above organizations each play a role in raising awareness, mobilizing activism and promoting policy change in Tulsa today.

Dialogue and Reconciliation. Community dialogue, truth-telling initiatives and reconciliation efforts are ongoing in Tulsa, bringing together residents from diverse backgrounds to confront historical injustices, address systemic racism and work toward a more inclusive and equitable future.

Police and Criminal Justice. Like many cities across the United States, Tulsa grapples with issues related to police-community relations, including concerns about racial profiling, excessive use of force and disparities in law enforcement practices. Efforts to improve transparency, accountability and community policing strategies are ongoing.

Criminal Justice Reform. There are continuing efforts in Tulsa to address racial disparities within the criminal justice system, including initiatives focused on bail reform, diversion programs and reducing mass incarceration. Community-led advocacy and policy changes aim to promote fairness and equity in the justice system.

Conclusion

The Tulsa Race Massacre of 1921 stands as a brutal reminder of the enduring consequences of racial violence and systemic injustice in American history. The destruction and devastation wrought during the Massacre, coupled with the lack of accountability and support from local and state governments, had far-reaching implications for generations to come.

Despite the passage of time, the legacy of the massacre continues to reverberate in contemporary Tulsa, shaping racial dynamics, socioeconomic disparities and ongoing efforts toward reconciliation and progress. Through grassroots activism, community engagement and advocacy for racial equity and social justice, organizations and individuals in Tulsa are working to confront the city's history of racial violence and build a more inclusive and equitable future.

CHAPTER SEVEN

THE DETROIT RACE RIOT OF 1943

The Detroit Race Riot of 1943 was one of the most violent racial conflicts in the United States during World War II. Like several riots discussed previously in this book, it occurred in a context of heightened racial tensions, economic pressures and demographic shifts. Following is a comprehensive overview of the causes, events and aftermath of the riot.

Background

In 1943, Detroit had become a became destination for Black families fleeing the South as part of the Great Migration. But among all northern cities, Detroit's wartime economy proved especially tempting. World War II had led to a boom in Detroit's industrial sector, especially in defense-related manufacturing. This economic boom attracted even more workers than in earlier years, both Black and White, leading to intense competition for jobs and housing.

Defense Manufacturing. During WWII, Detroit, known as the "Motor City," saw its automobile plants converted to producing military equipment. Companies like Ford, General Motors and Chrysler shifted their production to tanks, aircraft and other war materials. For example, the Ford Motor Company's Willow Run plant was famous for mass-producing B-24 Liberator bombers.

Arsenal of Democracy. President Franklin D. Roosevelt referred to Detroit as the "Arsenal of Democracy" due to its pivotal role in manufacturing war supplies. This label underscored the city's crucial contribution to the Allied war effort.

The wartime manufacturing boom created a surge in employment opportunities. Factories operated around the clock, requiring a vast workforce. This economic boom drew thousands of new workers of all backgrounds to the city, seeking jobs in the defense industry.

Influx of Workers. The Second Great Migration (roughly 1941 to 1970) saw a significant number of Black people move from the rural South to Northern cities like Detroit, seeking better job opportunities and escaping Jim Crow laws. The promise of steady, well-paying industrial jobs in Detroit was a powerful pull factor. Concurrently, White workers from other parts of the United States also flocked to Detroit seeking to benefit from the economic opportunities provided by the wartime industrial boom.

Black Employment. The war industries in Detroit employed a significant number of Black workers, often for lower wages and in less desirable or more dangerous positions compared to their White counterparts. Discrimination in hiring and promotions led to frequent disputes.

Packard Motor Car Company. One notable incident occurred at the Packard Motor Car Company in 1943 when the company promoted three Black workers to positions that had previously been held exclusively by White workers. This decision led to a strike by White workers, which quickly turned violent. To make the situation worse, Packard encouraged Black people to cross the strike lines of White workers, often resulting in shouts of racial slurs and threats of violence against Black "scabs."

The Sojourner Truth Housing Project. Another example is the Sojourner Truth Housing Project. The Project was a federal housing initiative intended to provide accommodation for Black defense workers. However, it faced fierce opposition from White residents in the area. In 1942, when Black families began moving into the Project, violent clashes ensued. White mobs protested, leading to physical confrontations, and police were called in to control the violence.

Segregated and Overcrowded Streetcars. As the population surged, Detroit's public transportation system became overwhelmed. Black residents often faced segregation and were forced to stand or sit in designated areas on streetcars and buses. The competition for seats and the necessity of public transport for commuting to war industry jobs led to frequent altercations.

School Overcrowding. The influx of new residents led to overcrowded schools, with Black children often being forced into underfunded and overcrowded schools due to segregation policies. In contrast, White schools, though also overcrowded, typically received better resources.

Access to Recreation Facilities. Black and White public recreation areas were usually segregated with the Black resources being typically much less desirable than those allocated for White people. This unequal allocation of public recreation areas is illustrated by the Belle Isle Incident.

Belle Isle, a popular recreational area in Detroit, was a frequent site of racial confrontations. On June 20, 1943, a fight broke out between Black and White youths on Belle Isle, escalating into a riot that spread into the city. The underlying cause was competition for access to the limited recreational facilities on the island.

(More details on the Belle Isle incident later in this Chapter.)

Redlining. The practice of redlining started in the 1930s and was institutionalized in Detroit by government policies and private sector practices. Here's a detailed look at how redlining began and evolved in Detroit:

Creation of the HOLC. In 1933, during the Great Depression, the U.S. government established the Home Owners' Loan Corporation (HOLC) as part of the New Deal to refinance home mortgages in default to prevent foreclosure.

HOLC created "residential security maps" of major American cities, including Detroit. These maps graded neighborhoods from A (best) to D (hazardous) based on perceived lending risk. The grades were color-coded, with "D" areas outlined in red, hence the term "redlining."

HOLC graded neighborhoods on factors such as housing quality, economic stability and racial composition. Areas with a higher percentage of Black residents or immigrants were often rated as high-risk, regardless of the actual financial stability of the residents.

FHA Adoption of HOLC Maps. Established in 1934, the Federal Housing Administration (FHA) adopted the HOLC's maps and risk assessments to guide its mortgage insurance program. It endorsed racial segregation by promoting racial covenants and refusing to insure mortgages in or near predominantly Black neighborhoods.

The FHA's underwriting manual explicitly recommended racial segregation and warned against the presence of "inharmonious racial groups" in neighborhoods.

Adoption by Private Lenders. Private banks and mortgage lenders were quick to adopt the HOLC's and FHA's guidelines, systematically denying loans to residents in redlined areas. This practice effectively institutionalized discrimination across the financial industry.

Adoption by Real Estate Professionals. Real estate agents and developers followed the same guidelines, perpetuating racial segregation by steering Black buyers away from White neighborhoods and enforcing racially restrictive covenants.

Racially Restrictive Covenants. Legal agreements known as Restrictive Covenants prevented Black people from buying or renting homes in certain areas. This legal discrimination reinforced residential segregation and stoked resentment among Black people. Efforts by Black residents to move into better housing in predominantly White neighborhoods were often met with violent resistance.

Law Enforcement. The Detroit police force was overwhelmingly White in a city with a large and increasing Black population. Black residents frequently faced harassment and discrimination from White police officers. Stop-and-frisk tactics, unjustified searches and aggressive interrogations were common experiences for many Black residents, especially Black men.

Reports of police violence were commonplace and widespread. Some officers were known to use excessive force during arrests and detentions, often without any provocation.

Incidents of Police Brutality. Specific incidents of police brutality sometimes garnered public attention, although many were swept under the rug. For instance, there were numerous documented cases where Black individuals were severely beaten or even killed by police. Examples include:

The Sweet Trials (1925-1926). Dr. Ossian Sweet, a Black physician, moved into a predominantly White neighborhood with his family. A violent White mob gathered outside his home, throwing stones and threatening Dr. Sweet's home.

Police were present but did little to disperse the mob. The situation escalated when allegedly "self-defense" shots were fired from inside the Sweet home, resulting in the death of one White man and injury to another. The police arrested Dr. Sweet, his family and friends, charging them with murder.

The case highlighted racial hostility and the police's failure to protect Black residents. It ended in two mistrials and was a significant moment in the fight against racial injustice.

Hastings Street Incident (1933). Located in Detroit's Black Bottom neighborhood, Hastings Street was a central thoroughfare known for its vibrant Black-owned businesses, cultural institutions and entertainment venues. It was a bustling area that served as a hub for Detroit's Black community during the early to mid-20th century.

Black Bottom was named for its rich, dark soil and was home to a predominantly Black population. It was a focal point for Black culture, social life, and economic activity in Detroit.

There were multiple documented instances of police brutality in the area. One particularly notable incident involved a police raid on a club, which led to several Black residents being beaten and arrested without cause. Such incidents were part of a broader pattern of systemic discrimination and violence by law enforcement against the Black community.

Protests and Complaints. Black residents and leaders frequently lodged complaints against police brutality and called for investigations and reforms. However, these complaints were often ignored or dismissed by city officials and police leadership, further intensifying the sense of injustice.

Mistrust and Anger. The continuous cycle of police violence and lack of accountability led to deep-seated mistrust and anger towards the police within the Black community. This sentiment was exacerbated by the perception that the police were an occupying force rather than protectors of public safety.

Trigger Incidents

Belle Isle Incident. As previously mentioned, on June 20, 1943, a hot summer day, large numbers of people, both Black and White, gathered at Belle Isle, a popular island park in the Detroit River. The park was one of the few places where Black people could gather in significant numbers.

In the evening, a fight broke out between groups of Black and White youths on the Belle Isle Bridge, which connects the island to the mainland. As police attempted to break up the altercation, false rumors began to spread. One rumor claimed that a Black man had raped a White woman on the bridge; another rumor, spreading within the Black community, claimed that White sailors had killed a Black woman and her baby. These rumors inflamed existing racial tensions and led to direct physical violence on the bridge.

The rioting quicky spilled over to the predominantly Black Paradise Valley neighborhood. White mobs attacked the homes and businesses of Black residents, and in retaliation, Black residents defended their neighborhood, resulting in widespread violence. Numerous Black-owned businesses, homes and properties were looted and destroyed. White rioters set fires and smashed windows.

The Riot

As the violence grew and spread, the Detroit police, who were predominantly White, were overwhelmed by the scale of the violence. There were reports of police brutality and racial bias, with many accusations that the police were either ineffective or actively contributing to the violence against Black residents.

National Guard Deployed. On June 21, 1943, as the riots escalated, Michigan Governor Harry Kelly mobilized the National Guard to assist in quelling the violence. The number of Guardsmen deployed is the subject of differing opinions among historians. However, it is clear that significant Guard troops arrived in Detroit midday on the 21st.

Federal Assistance. By evening, Governor Kelly remained dissatisfied with the continuing violence in Detroit and called U.S President, Franklin D. Roosevelt, for assistance. Roosevelt approved the deployment of 6,000 federal troops, including additional National Guard units, who arrived in Detroit on June 2nd.

The mere presence of armed National Guard troops and federal soldiers was a show of force that functioned as a deterrent to further violence. Additionally, Guard troops and federal soldiers conducted patrols throughout the city to maintain order and prevent further outbreaks of violence. They secured key locations, such as government buildings, infrastructure and critical facilities.

Troops also protect citizens, homes, businesses and other properties from looting, arson and destruction, guarding vulnerable areas and providing much-welcomed security to residents who remained in their homes.

Riot Control Tactics. Detroit police deployed tear gas canisters to disperse crowds and discourage rioters from congregating in specific areas. Mounted police units, consisting of officers on horseback, joined the troops to assist in patrolling riot-affected areas and maintaining order.

Riot Ends. By midnight on June 22nd, the rioting had substantially dissipated, and relative calm returned to Detroit's streets.

Immediate Impact

Casualties. Various accounts suggest that anywhere from 34 to 43 individuals lost their lives during the riots, while hundreds more sustained injuries. The casualties included both civilians and law enforcement personnel, reflecting the widespread violence and chaos that engulfed the city during the unrest.

Over 1,800 people were arrested during the riots, with the majority being Black.

Property Damage. The riots resulted in widespread destruction of property, including businesses, homes and public infrastructure. Many Black neighborhoods, particularly on the east side of Detroit, were heavily affected. Rioters also targeted both Black and White-owned businesses, leading to extensive looting and arson.

The estimated dollar value of property damage during the 1943 Detroit riots is estimated at up to $2 million (approximately $40 million in today's dollars).

Long-term Effects

Civil Rights Movement. The Detroit Riot of 1943 highlighted the urgent need for civil rights reforms and the protection of Black communities. It became a rallying point for civil rights activists who sought to address racial discrimination and police brutality.

Urban Segregation. The riot reinforced patterns of residential segregation in Detroit. Black people were often confined to overcrowded and under-resourced neighborhoods, facing ongoing discrimination in housing and employment.

Historical Memory. The Detroit Race Riot of 1943 is remembered as a pivotal event in the history of racial violence in the United States. It is studied as part of the broader context of racial tensions and civil rights struggles during World War II.

Cultural Impact. The riot has been the subject of numerous books, documentaries and scholarly studies. It serves as a reminder of the destructive power of racial hatred and the importance of addressing systemic racism.

Commemoration. Efforts have been made to commemorate the victims and educate the public about the riot. These include historical markers, educational programs and community events aimed at promoting racial understanding and reconciliation.

Detroit Today

Income Disparities. Detroit's population in 2024 is approximately 78.6% Black and 9.8% White. Despite the advantage in numbers of people, Detroit's median household income favors White people, who receive approximately $46,621 per year for a median household, versus Black median households who only receive $34,844 per year.

Economic Inequality. Overall, economic inequality along racial lines favoring White people remains a pressing issue in Detroit. Black residents disproportionately experience poverty, unemployment and lack of access to quality jobs and economic opportunities. Persistent racial disparities in wealth and homeownership contribute to socioeconomic inequality and perpetuate systemic barriers to upward mobility.

Housing Segregation. Segregation in housing continues to impact Detroit, with patterns of residential segregation shaping access to housing, neighborhood quality and community resources. And one can still observe the impacts of redlining and racial restrictive covenants on the city map.

Education. Disparities in educational opportunities also persist in Detroit, with Black students disproportionately attending underfunded schools and facing barriers to academic achievement. Segregation in the public school system, along with inadequate resources, contribute to educational inequities and perpetuate the cycle of poverty and disadvantage for many Black youth.

<u>Criminal Justice.</u> Racial disparities in the criminal justice system remain a significant concern in Detroit, as in many other cities across the United States. Black people are disproportionately impacted by policing practices, arrest rates and incarceration rates, reflecting systemic biases and discriminatory policies. Efforts to address racial profiling, police brutality and mass incarceration remain ongoing.

But not all the news is unfavorable.

<u>Political Representation.</u> Detroit has seen an increase in Black political representation at various levels of government, including city council members, state legislators and congressional representatives. This representation can help address the needs and priorities of the Black community and advocate for policies that promote equity and justice.

<u>Community Initiatives.</u> Numerous community-led initiatives and grassroots organizations in Detroit focus on empowering Black residents, addressing systemic barriers and promoting social and economic justice. Organizations like Detroit Action and the Detroit People's Platform empower Black residents by providing advocacy, organizing and leadership development opportunities. These initiatives provide support services, advocacy and resources to empower individuals and communities to advocate for change and improve their quality of life.

<u>Economic Development.</u> There has been increased investment in economic development initiatives aimed at revitalizing neighborhoods, creating jobs and fostering entrepreneurship within the Black community. Examples include:

Motor City Match. Established in 2015, Motor City Match is a program launched by the City of Detroit that provides grants, loans and technical assistance to small businesses and entrepreneurs, particularly those located in underserved neighborhoods. The program aims to stimulate economic growth, create jobs and revitalize commercial corridors by supporting the development of new businesses and the expansion of existing ones owned by people of color.

Detroit Development Fund. Established in 1998, the Detroit Development Fund is a nonprofit organization that provides financing and technical assistance to small businesses, real estate developers and community organizations in Detroit. DDF offers loans, equity investments and other financial products to support projects that promote economic development, affordable housing and neighborhood revitalization, with a focus on minority-owned businesses and underserved communities.

Build Institute. Established in 2012, Build Institute is a nonprofit organization that offers entrepreneurship training, mentorship and support services to aspiring entrepreneurs in Detroit. The organization's programs, such as the Build Basics entrepreneurship course and the Co.Starters business accelerator program, provide participants with the skills, resources and networks needed to start and grow successful businesses. Build Institute prioritizes supporting entrepreneurs from underrepresented backgrounds, including Black, Indigenous and people of color (BIPOC) communities.

The Greening of Detroit. Established in 1989, The Greening of Detroit is a nonprofit organization dedicated to revitalizing Detroit's neighborhoods through tree planting, urban agriculture and environmental stewardship initiatives. The organization's programs, such as the Detroit Conservation Corps and the Urban Roots Youth Farm, provide job training, workforce development and employment opportunities for residents, particularly those from low-income and minority communities. By engaging residents in community greening projects, The Greening of Detroit promotes economic empowerment, environmental sustainability and neighborhood revitalization.

TechTown Detroit. TechTown Detroit is a nonprofit business incubator and entrepreneurial support organization that fosters innovation and economic development in Detroit's technology and startup ecosystem. The organization offers coworking space, business acceleration programs and mentorship opportunities for tech startups and small businesses, with a focus on supporting minority-owned and women-owned enterprises.

TechTown's programs, such as the Retail Boot Camp and the DTX Launch Detroit accelerator, provide resources and support to entrepreneurs from diverse backgrounds, helping them launch and scale successful ventures in the city.

Educational Equity Efforts. Efforts to promote educational equity and improve outcomes for Black students in Detroit schools are underway. Initiatives focused on expanding access to quality education, reducing disparities in academic achievement and providing support services to students and families aim to address systemic barriers and promote academic success.

<u>Policing.</u> There are ongoing efforts to improve police-community relations and promote accountability and transparency in law enforcement practices. Community policing initiatives, de-escalation training, deployment of body cameras and efforts to address racial bias in policing aim to build trust and foster positive relationships between law enforcement agencies and the Black community.

<u>Cultural Heritage.</u> Detroit has a rich cultural heritage and a vibrant arts and music scene that celebrates Black culture and history. Cultural preservation efforts, community events and artistic expressions contribute to a sense of pride, identity and resilience within the Black community.

<u>Civil Rights Organizations.</u> Detroit is home to various civil rights organizations, advocacy groups and community-based initiatives that work to address racial injustice, promote equity and empower marginalized communities. These organizations play a vital role in advocating for policy reforms, providing support services and fostering community resilience. Following are a few examples:

<u>Detroit NAACP.</u> The Detroit branch of the NAACP is dedicated to fighting for civil rights, social justice and racial equality in the city. The organization advocates for policies and programs that address systemic racism, promote economic empowerment and protect the rights of marginalized communities. The Detroit NAACP also provides legal assistance, voter education and community outreach services to empower residents and promote civic engagement.

Detroit Justice Center. Established in 2018, the Detroit Justice Center is a nonprofit legal advocacy organization that works to dismantle the criminal justice system's disparate impact on low-income communities of color in Detroit. The organization provides legal representation, advocacy and policy research to address issues such as mass incarceration, racial profiling and police brutality. The Detroit Justice Center also offers reentry support services to formerly incarcerated individuals and advocates for alternatives to incarceration that prioritize rehabilitation and community-based solutions.

Detroit Action. Established in 2019, Detroit Action is a grassroots organization that organizes community members to advocate for social, economic and racial justice in Detroit. The organization focuses on issues such as affordable housing, environmental justice and workers' rights, mobilizing residents to take collective action and hold elected officials accountable. Detroit Action also provides leadership development, training and support to empower individuals and communities to advocate for change and build power.

Detroit People's Platform. Established in 2013, the Detroit People's Platform is a coalition of community organizations, activists and residents working to advance social and economic justice in Detroit. The organization advocates for policies and investments that prioritize the needs of low-income communities, people of color and marginalized populations. The Detroit People's Platform engages in community organizing, policy advocacy and grassroots campaigns to address issues such as housing affordability, public transportation, and environmental equity.

Michigan United. Established in 2012, Michigan United is a statewide coalition of organizations and individuals working to promote social, economic and racial justice in Michigan. The organization's Detroit chapter focuses on issues such as immigrant rights, environmental justice and racial equity, mobilizing residents to take collective action and advocate for change.

Economic Development and Opportunity. Promoting economic development and creating pathways to opportunity for all residents is critical for addressing racial disparities and advancing racial equity in Detroit. Initiatives focused on job creation, workforce development, small business support and equitable economic growth can help address systemic barriers and create more inclusive pathways to prosperity.

Conclusion

The Detroit Race Riot of 1943 presents a somber reminder of the deep-seated racial tensions, economic disparities and systemic injustices that have plagued American cities throughout history. Fueled by discrimination, economic competition and police brutality, the riot underscored the urgent need for civil rights reforms and social justice initiatives.

While the riot resulted in tragic loss of life and widespread destruction, it also served as a catalyst for change, galvanizing civil rights activists and community leaders to advocate for equality and justice.

Today, Detroit continues to grapple with racial disparities and segregation, but there are signs of progress and resilience. Increasing Black political representation, community empowerment initiatives and economic development efforts demonstrate a commitment to addressing systemic barriers and promoting equity.

As Detroit confronts its past and works towards a more inclusive and equitable future, the lessons of the 1943 Riot serve as a powerful reminder of the ongoing struggle for racial justice and the importance of collective action in building a more equitable society.

CHAPTER EIGHT
THE WATTS RIOTS OF 1965

The Watts Riots of 1965, also known as the Watts Rebellion, were a significant event in the history of civil unrest in the United States. The riots occurred in the predominantly Black neighborhood of Watts in the city of Los Angeles, California, and were driven by a combination of systemic issues and immediate triggers. Following is a detailed overview.

Background

Segregation and Discrimination. Despite enactment of the Civil Rights Act of 1964, Black people in Los Angeles still faced systemic racism in 1965, including police brutality, employment discrimination, inadequate housing and poor educational opportunities.

Economic Disparities. The Black community in Watts was plagued by high unemployment rates, poverty and limited access to economic opportunities, leading to widespread frustration and discontent. Causes of these disparities include the following:

Limited Job Opportunities. Despite the booming post-war economy in other parts of Los Angeles, Watts residents faced high unemployment rates due to discrimination and limited access to jobs. Many businesses in Los Angeles either did not hire Black people or relegated them to low-paying, menial jobs.

Industrial Decline. Watts was hit hard by the post-war decline in manufacturing jobs, which had previously provided employment opportunities to many Black people. The shift from industrial to service-oriented jobs further marginalized the community, as these new jobs often required skills and education that were less accessible to residents of Watts.

Low Incomes. The lack of well-paying jobs contributed to high levels of poverty in Watts. Many families lived below the poverty line, struggling to afford basic necessities such as food, housing and healthcare.

Overcrowded Housing. Economic constraints led to overcrowded living conditions. Many families were forced to share small, substandard housing units, which exacerbated health and social issues.

Poor Infrastructure. The Watts neighborhood suffered from inadequate infrastructure, including poorly maintained roads, limited public transportation and insufficient public services such as sanitation and emergency response.

Educational Disparities. Schools in Watts were underfunded and overcrowded, providing inferior education compared to schools in wealthier, predominantly White neighborhoods. This educational gap limited the economic opportunities available to young people growing up in Watts.

Lack of Investment. There was also a significant lack of investment in the community. Businesses were reluctant to open in Watts due to perceptions of crime and instability, and there were few initiatives to foster economic development within the neighborhood.

Discriminatory Lending Practices. Banks and lending institutions often practiced redlining, refusing to offer loans or mortgages to Black people in certain neighborhoods, including Watts. This made it difficult for residents to buy homes or start businesses, perpetuating economic disenfranchisement.

Police-Community Relations. On top of all these challenging conditions, Black people also reported numerous incidents of police brutality. The Los Angeles Police Department (LAPD) had a notorious reputation for racial profiling and brutality against Black people. In fact, police brutality against Black people (and Mexican Americans) in Los Angeles was prevalent both before and after the Civil Rights Act of 1964. Here are some examples from that time period:

The Bloody Christmas Incident (1951). The Bloody Christmas incident occurred on December 25, 1951, when a group of LAPD officers engaged in a violent rampage against Mexican American and Black youths in downtown Los Angeles. The officers beat and arrested numerous young men, resulting in injuries and several deaths.

The Sleepy Lagoon Murder Trial (1942). The Sleepy Lagoon Murder Trial was a high-profile case involving the wrongful conviction of a group of young Mexican American men for the murder of another young man near a swimming hole known as Sleepy Lagoon. The trial was marked by systemic racism, police misconduct and the use of coerced confessions.

The Zoot Suit Riots (1943). The Zoot Suit Riots were a series of racially motivated attacks against Mexican American and Black youths in Los Angeles in June 1943. The riots were fueled by tensions between White servicemen stationed in the city during World War II and minority youth who wore distinctive clothing styles known as "zoot suits." The LAPD failed to intervene effectively, and in some cases, officers targeted and assaulted minority youths instead of protecting them from violence.

Even outside of specific incidents, the LAPD had a long history of discriminatory practices and excessive force targeting Black communities. Documented incidents of racial profiling, harassment and unwarranted use of violence were common, creating an environment of fear and mistrust among Black residents.

Ample evidence indicates that Los Angeles Police targeted motorists for stops based on racial profiling rather than legitimate suspicion of wrongdoing, resulting in a constant fear of being pulled over in the minds of Black residents. In addition, such stops often led to unwarranted searches, harassment and sometimes physical violence during encounters with police officers.

Documented instances of police officers using excessive force against Black people were not uncommon. These included physical beatings during arrests, often justified under the pretext of resisting arrest.

Neighborhoods with predominantly Black populations, such as Watts and other South Los Angeles communities, were subjected to more aggressive policing tactics compared to predominantly White neighborhoods. Such policies included higher rates of arrests, citations and police presence.

Justice System. Furthermore, there was a total absence of effective mechanisms for holding police officers accountable for misconduct or abuses of power. Complaints filed by Black residents regarding police brutality or discriminatory treatment were often dismissed or ignored.

Trigger Incident

It was a low-key traffic stop around 7 p.m. on a Wednesday evening that ignited what would become known as the Watts Rebellion. This incident tells a tale of how one action leads to another until chaos results.

August 11, 1965, stepbrothers Marquette and Ronald Frye were pulled over by a White California Highway Patrol (CHP) officer while driving their mother's car near the corner of Avalon Boulevard and 116th Street in the Watts neighborhood of Los Angeles.

Marquette failed a sobriety test and panicked as he was arrested. As Marquette's anger rose at the thought of going to jail, a scuffle broke out between him and one of the police officers. Ronald joined in, partly to protest the arrest but also to protect his brother.

A crowd began to gather, and back-up police arrived under the assumption that the crowd was hostile, which resulted in a fight between someone in the crowd and an officer. Another newly arrived officer jabbed Ronald in the stomach with his riot baton and then moved to intervene in the fight between Marquette and the officer attempting to arrest him.

Marquette was knocked down by the riot baton, after which police applied handcuffs and placed him in the back seat of their police car. The Frye brothers' mother, Rena, showed up on the scene and—believing police were abusing Marquette—rushed to pull the officers off him, resulting in another fight.

The police then arrested Rena and forced her into the car, followed by Ronald, who had been handcuffed after attempting to intervene peacefully in his stepmother's arrest.

As the crowd got angrier about the scene they were witnessing, more highway patrol officers arrived and used batons and brandished shotguns to keep the crowd back from the police car. Hundreds more residents flocked to the scene to investigate the sirens there.

As two motorcycle police attempted to leave, someone in the Black crowd spat on him. Those police stopped to pursue the woman who they believed was responsible, but the crowd converged around them, prompting several other officers into the crowd to assist their fellow officers. More police cars were called to the scene.

The two motorcycle police eventually found Joyce Ann Gaines and arrested her for spitting at them. She resisted and was dragged out of the crowd which, believing she was pregnant, became even angrier.

The Riots

By 7.45 p.m., the riot was in full force, with rocks, bottles and more being thrown at civilian buses and cars that had been stalled in traffic because of the escalating incident.

The unrest quickly spread from the site of the arrest to the surrounding neighborhood.

Over the next six days, the violence intensified dramatically. Thousands of Black people took to the streets, looting and burning businesses and clashing with police.

On August 13, 1965, two days after the riots began, California Governor Pat Brown deployed approximately 14,000 National Guard troops to help restore order and assist local law enforcement in quelling the violence and unrest.

Governor Brown also requested assistance from President Lyndon B. Johnson, but Johnson decided that the local police and Guard troops could manage without federal intervention. No federal troops were ever sent.

After six days of violence and chaos, the combination of Guard intervention, increased law enforcement presence, community outreach efforts and public fatigue with the violence and destruction contributed to the eventual end of the Watts Riots on August 17th, 1965.

Immediate Impact

The Watts Riots of 1965 had profound and far-reaching impacts on the community, the city of Los Angeles and the broader civil rights movement in the United States. Following are some of the key impacts:

Casualties. The riots resulted in 34 deaths, over 1,000 injuries and nearly 4,000 arrests. The vast majority of both deaths and arrests were of Black people. Some White people died, including both civilians and law enforcement. The exact number remains uncertain, but the total was much smaller than Black people.

Property Damage. The riots resulted in extensive property damage, with estimates of up to $40 million (equivalent to over $300 million today). Hundreds of buildings were damaged or destroyed, including homes, businesses and public facilities.

As the epicenter of the riots, Watts experienced the most significant destruction. Numerous buildings were burned or looted, including homes, small businesses and public facilities.

Jordan High School. Jordan High School, located in the heart of Watts, experienced significant damage. While the school itself was not completely destroyed, parts of the building were vandalized, and equipment and supplies were looted or burned.

The Watts Happening Cultural Center. The Watts Happening Cultural Center, which was a hub for cultural and social activities in Watts, was vandalized and partially burned.

The Watts Branch Library. The Watts Branch Library sustained damage during the riots, including broken windows, vandalism and theft of books and equipment.

The Watts Health Center. The Watts Health Center, which provided medical services to the community, was vandalized and looted. Medical equipment and supplies were stolen or destroyed.

Social Services Department. The local office of the Department of Social Services, which provided welfare and other assistance programs, was also targeted during the riots. The building was vandalized, and records and equipment were damaged or destroyed.

Other Areas Affected. South Central Los Angeles, adjacent to Watts, also saw extensive property damage and looting. Businesses along major thoroughfares like Central Avenue and Avalon Boulevard were particularly hard hit. Many stores that served as essential services for the Black community were destroyed. Several mixed-use buildings, which housed businesses on the ground floor and residential units above, were set on fire.

Compton, another predominantly Black neighborhood, experienced significant rioting and property destruction. Many retail stores, including supermarkets and pharmacies, were looted and burned, disrupting access to essential goods and services.

National Awareness. The riots drew national and international attention to the issues of racial inequality, police brutality and economic disparity in Black communities. It highlighted the urgent need for civil rights reforms.

Government Response. Partially in response to the Watts Rebellion, President Lyndon B. Johnson established the National Advisory Commission on Civil Disorders (also known as the Kerner Commission) to investigate the causes of the unrest and provide recommendations to prevent future occurrences.

Kerner Commission Report. The Kerner Commission's report concluded that the nation was "moving toward two societies, one Black, one White—separate and unequal." It identified systemic racism, economic inequality and inadequate housing, education and employment opportunities as root causes of urban unrest. The report constituted a wake-up call to many American citizens and politicians.

The report called for comprehensive federal initiatives to address racial disparities, improve urban infrastructure and enhance social services. It also emphasized the need for better community relations and policing reforms.

Civil Rights Movement. The Watts Riots galvanized civil rights activists and organizations, providing momentum for continued advocacy for social justice and equality. It particularly underscored the urgency of addressing systemic issues faced by Black communities.

The riots also shifted the focus of the civil rights movement to include urban poverty and economic inequality, broadening the agenda beyond desegregation and voting rights.

Law Enforcement Reforms. The riots prompted local and state authorities to reevaluate policing practices, leading to some reforms aimed at improving community relations and reducing instances of police brutality.

Increased Tensions. Despite some efforts at reform, tensions between the LAPD and Black communities remained high, with ongoing reports of discrimination and excessive force in the following years.

Long-Term Effects

Persistent Inequality. Many of the underlying issues that contributed to the Watts Riots, such as poverty, unemployment, biased policing and inadequate housing, persisted for decades.

Despite these challenges, the community of Watts demonstrated resilience and strength, with local leaders and organizations working to rebuild and advocate for better conditions.

Cultural and Historical Significance. The Watts Riots are remembered as a pivotal moment in American history, reflecting the deep-seated racial tensions and systemic inequities that existed in urban centers. The riots highlighted the need for comprehensive social and economic reforms.

Ongoing Relevance. The issues that sparked the Watts Riots—police brutality, economic inequality and racial discrimination—remain relevant today. The riots are often referenced in discussions about racial justice and the continuing struggle for civil rights in the United States.

Watts Today

Systemic racism disadvantaging Black residents of Watts continues to present a challenge in 2024. Although statistical information on income is not available on a neighborhood basis, statistics for the entire city of Los Angeles are relevant. In 2024, median White households in Los Angeles received White $97,663 per year in income, while median Black households received only $51,940.

As of recent data, the racial composition of the neighborhood of Watts in Los Angeles, CA is predominantly Hispanic or Latino, with a significant Black population. Following is an approximate breakdown.

Hispanic or Latino. Approximately 70-75%

African American. Approximately 20-25%

Other Races (including White, Asian and Native American). Approximately 5%

These figures reflect the demographic changes over the years, with a substantial increase in the Hispanic or Latino population and a decline in the Black population since the mid-20th century.

Housing Segregation. Despite efforts to desegregate, many neighborhoods in Los Angeles remain racially and economically segregated. Historical practices like redlining have long-lasting effects, contributing to disparities in home ownership rates and property values between different racial groups.

Gentrification. Rapid gentrification in areas such as Downtown LA and parts of South LA has led to the displacement of long-time residents, often from communities of color, exacerbating economic and racial inequalities.

School Funding. Public schools in Los Angeles are funded by local property taxes, leading to significant disparities in funding and resources between schools in affluent, predominantly White neighborhoods and those in lower-income, predominantly Black and Latino neighborhoods.

Achievement Gap. There is a persistent achievement gap between White students and students of color, with Black and Latino students often having lower graduation rates and standardized test scores.

Job Opportunities. Black residents of Los Angeles face higher unemployment rates and are often concentrated in lower-wage jobs with fewer opportunities for advancement compared to their White counterparts.

Wage Gap. There is a notable wage gap, with Black workers earning significantly less than White workers on average.

<u>Access to Healthcare.</u> Even in 2024, communities of color in Los Angeles often have less access to quality healthcare facilities and services, leading to disparities in health outcomes. This was particularly evident during the COVID-19 pandemic, which disproportionately affected Black communities.

<u>Health Disparities.</u> Higher rates of chronic diseases, such as diabetes and hypertension, are found among Black and Latino populations in LA, due to a combination of genetic, environmental and socioeconomic factors.

<u>Police Practices.</u> According to data from the Los Angeles Police Department (LAPD), Black communities face a higher frequency of traffic stops, pedestrian stops and searches, often without evidence of wrongdoing.

Arrest rates for Black individuals are also significantly higher than those for White people. These disparities are often linked to over-policing in predominantly Black neighborhoods, leading to a cycle of criminalization and incarceration, which in turn leads to a decrease in employability.

Examples underscore the continuing policing problems:

<u>The Case of Dijon Kizzee.</u> In August 2020, Dijon Kizzee, a 29-year-old Black man, was shot and killed by Los Angeles County sheriff's deputies in South Los Angeles.

The incident occurred when deputies attempted to stop Kizzee for an alleged bicycle code violation while he was riding his bike in the Westmont neighborhood of South Los Angeles. According to the sheriff's department, Kizzee dropped his bike and ran away from the deputies.

The deputies pursued Kizzee on foot. During the chase, Kizzee reportedly dropped some clothing items he was carrying. The deputies claimed that among these items was a handgun, which Kizzee allegedly picked up.

The deputies stated that when Kizzee bent down to pick up the handgun, they opened fire, shooting him 16 times, including multiple shots in the back. Kizzee was pronounced dead at the scene. According to the Los Angeles County Sheriff's Department, a handgun was found at the scene where Dijon Kizzee was shot and killed. Some witnesses dispute this fact.

The Killing of Andres Guardado. On the evening of June 18th, 2020, Andres Guardado was working as an unofficial security guard at an auto body shop. According to the Los Angeles County Sheriff's Department, two deputies from the Compton station were on patrol when they noticed Guardado talking to someone in a car that was blocking the entrance to the shop.

The deputies claimed that Guardado looked at them, produced a handgun, and ran away. One deputy pursued Guardado on foot into an alleyway next to the auto body shop.

According to the deputies' account, the deputy caught up with Guardado in the alley, and during the encounter, the deputy fired six shots, hitting Guardado five times in the back. Guardado was pronounced dead at the scene.

The sheriff's department stated that a .40-caliber semiautomatic pistol with an extended magazine was found at the scene and alleged that Guardado had been carrying it. However, this claim has been disputed by Guardado's family and their attorneys, who argue that he was not known to carry a weapon and that he posed no threat to the deputies.

At the time of the shooting, Los Angeles County sheriff's deputies were not equipped with body cameras, which has complicated efforts to independently verify the details of the incident.

The Death of Valentina Orellana-Peralta. On December 23, 2021, LAPD officers responded to a report of an armed robbery at a Burlington store in North Hollywood. The officers encountered a suspect, who allegedly fired at them inside the store.

During the exchange of gunfire between the suspect and the officers, a stray bullet struck 14-year-old Valentina Orellana-Peralta, who was in a dressing room with her mother inside the store. Valentina was hit by the bullet and sustained critical injuries.

Valentina was rushed to the hospital in critical condition but tragically succumbed to her injuries shortly after arrival.

Wealth Gap. Los Angeles also features a significant wealth gap between White residents and residents of color, influenced primarily by historical and ongoing discrimination in housing, employment and access to capital.

Positive Initiatives. Despite ongoing challenges, there are several positive initiatives and efforts in Los Angeles aimed at addressing systemic racism and promoting racial equity:

Grassroots Organizations. Community organizations such as Black Lives Matter Los Angeles (BLM LA), Community Coalition, and InnerCity Struggle continue to advocate for systemic change through grassroots organizing, community empowerment and policy advocacy.

Youth Leadership Programs. Organizations like Brotherhood Crusade and Youth Justice Coalition provide leadership development programs for youth of color, empowering them to advocate for social justice and equity in their communities.

Ethnic Studies Programs. Los Angeles Unified School District (LAUSD) has expanded its ethnic studies curriculum to include more diverse perspectives and histories, helping students learn about the contributions and experiences of various racial and ethnic groups.

Anti-Racism Training. Many institutions, including schools, businesses, and government agencies, are implementing anti-racism training programs to educate staff and community members about systemic racism and promote inclusive practices.

Measure J. Passed by voters in November 2020, Measure J mandates that a minimum of 10% of Los Angeles County's unrestricted general funds be allocated to community programs and alternatives to incarceration. This measure aims to address systemic inequalities and invest in underserved communities.

Police Reform Measures. Efforts are ongoing to reform policing practices in Los Angeles, including enhanced training on de-escalation techniques, community policing strategies and increased transparency in officer conduct through body-worn cameras and civilian oversight boards.

Affordable Housing Initiatives. Non-profit organizations and government agencies are collaborating to increase affordable housing options and prevent displacement in historically marginalized communities.

Support for Minority-Owned Businesses. Programs and initiatives support minority entrepreneurs and small business owners through access to capital, technical assistance and networking opportunities.

The Los Angeles Department of Consumer and Business Affairs (DCBA). The DCBA operates several BusinessSource Centers throughout Los Angeles. These centers provide free business consulting services, workshops and resources tailored to minority and underserved entrepreneurs.

The Minority Business Development Agency (MBDA) Business Center - Los Angeles. The MBDA, funded by the U.S. Department of Commerce, offers technical assistance and consulting services to minority-owned businesses. It provides help with access to contracts, capital and markets to foster growth and competitiveness.

Other Organizations. Various organizations like the Vermont Slauson Economic Development Corporation (VSEDC) and the Black Business Association (BBA) provide resources such as business loans, mentorship and networking opportunities specifically tailored to Black small business owners in Los Angeles.

Diversity in Lending. Union Bank offers a Business Diversity Lending Program designed to provide access to capital for minority-owned businesses. The program offers flexible lending options, technical assistance and financial education to help minority entrepreneurs succeed.

Equitable Healthcare Access. Healthcare providers and community health organizations are working to reduce health disparities among racial and ethnic minorities in Los Angeles through targeted outreach, culturally competent care and advocacy for healthcare reform.

Social Services Expansion. Expanded access to social services such as mental health support, substance abuse treatment and youth services aims to address systemic barriers and improve overall well-being in underserved communities.

California African American Museum. Organizations like the California African American Museum, established in 1977, celebrate and preserve the cultural heritage of diverse communities in Los Angeles. The museum focuses on the history, art and culture of African Americans, with a particular emphasis on California and the western United States. The museum hosts exhibitions, educational programs and events aimed at promoting a deeper understanding of African American heritage and contributions.

Conclusion

The Watts Riots of 1965 cast a spotlight illuminating the profound impact of systemic racism, economic inequality and police brutality on Black communities. Triggered by a routine traffic stop that escalated into widespread unrest, the riots exposed deep-seated grievances stemming from decades of discriminatory practices and neglect in Watts and beyond.

The aftermath of the riots brought both immediate and lasting effects. It prompted national awareness of racial inequality and spurred governmental responses, including the establishment of the Kerner Commission to investigate the riots' causes and recommend solutions. The commission's findings underscored systemic racism, economic disparities and inadequate social services as root causes of urban unrest, advocating for comprehensive reforms in housing, education, employment and policing.

Despite these efforts, many of the underlying issues that fueled the riots persist today. Communities like Watts continue to face challenges of economic hardship, educational disparities and disproportionate policing practices. The legacy of the Watts Riots resonates in ongoing struggles for racial justice and equality, highlighting the enduring need for systemic change and community empowerment.

CHAPTER NINE
THE NEWARK AND DETROIT RIOTS (1967)

The Newark and Detroit Riots of 1967 were two of the most significant and destructive episodes of civil unrest in the United States during the 1960s. Both riots were part of the broader wave of racial disturbances that erupted across the country during what came to be known as the "Long Hot Summer" of 1967. Following is a detailed overview of each event, their causes, key incidents and aftermaths.

Newark Riot (July 12-17, 1967)

Background

Despite the enactment of the Civil Rights Act in 1964, systemic racism, well-entrenched discriminatory practices and unequal access to employment opportunities continued to plague Newark, New Jersey in 1967.

Employment Discrimination. As was true of many northern cities during the second Great Migration, many manufacturing plants and industrial facilities in Newark excluded Black people from skilled positions and managerial roles. Instead, Black workers were often relegated to unskilled, hazardous or labor-intensive jobs with lower wages and limited opportunities for advancement. Some companies or industries continued to segregate their workforces entirely.

Unions. White-only unions often dominated construction trades, effectively preventing Black workers from accessing well-paying jobs in carpentry, plumbing, electrical work and other skilled trades.

Even on those occasions when minority contractors were awarded construction contracts, they often faced challenges in hiring Black workers due to union resistance and discrimination within subcontracting networks.

Service Industry. In the service sector, Black people were disproportionately employed in lower-paying positions such as janitorial work, domestic service and food service. These jobs offered minimal job security, low wages and limited opportunities for career advancement.

Many service-oriented businesses, including hotels, restaurants and retail stores, maintained discriminatory hiring criteria that excluded Black people from customer-facing roles or positions requiring interaction with predominantly White clientele.

Public Employment. Black people in Newark also faced barriers to employment in local government agencies and public institutions. Civil service exams often contained cultural references, vocabulary and scenarios that were more familiar to White applicants who had received better educational opportunities and preparation. Study materials were also disproportionately more available to White than Black test-takers.

Educational Barriers. Discrimination in educational opportunities limited access for Black people to higher education, which in turn restricted their ability to pursue careers in professions such as law, medicine and finance.

Glass Ceiling. Even in industries where Black people managed to secure professional positions, they often encountered a "glass ceiling" that hindered their advancement to leadership roles and executive positions within organizations.

<u>Wage Gap.</u> Although reliable statistics are scant, historians generally recognize that, at the time, Black workers earned lower wages than their White counterparts for similar work. This wage gap contributed to higher levels of poverty and economic insecurity among Black families in Newark.

<u>Redlining Practices.</u> Banks and lending institutions engaged in redlining, a still-legal discriminatory practice that systematically denied mortgage loans and other financial services to Black communities. Redlining restricted Black families from buying homes and building wealth through property ownership.

<u>Segregation.</u> Black communities were confined primarily to impoverished areas of the city known as West Ward, South Ward and Central Ward. These neighborhoods featured substandard housing conditions and often lacked adequate infrastructure, public services and amenities compared to predominantly White areas.

<u>Underfunded Schools.</u> Due to exclusive use of property taxes to fund education, schools attended by Black students in Newark were typically underfunded and overcrowded compared to schools in predominantly White neighborhoods.

<u>Limited Business Ownership.</u> Black entrepreneurship in Newark was hindered by lack of access to capital, discriminatory lending practices and limited opportunities for business development and growth.

<u>Access to Healthcare.</u> Black people in Newark often faced barriers to accessing quality healthcare services, resulting in disparities in health outcomes and life expectancy. Hospitals and clinics were often located in predominantly White neighborhoods, making it difficult for Black residents to access essential medical services, especially in emergencies.

Hospitals and healthcare facilities frequently practiced discriminatory admission policies, refusing to admit Black patients or providing them with substandard care compared to White patients, contributing to disparities in health outcomes and treatment options.

Public Clinics. Public healthcare services in predominantly Black neighborhoods of Newark were often underfunded and understaffed, resulting in longer wait times for appointments, limited availability of medical supplies and equipment and inadequate support for chronic health conditions.

Social Services. Social welfare programs and public assistance were insufficient to meet the needs of Black families who, owing to racial discrimination and its effects, were struggling with poverty, housing instability and unemployment.

Discriminator Policing. Reports indicate that Newark had policing issues like those experienced by residents of Watts. Uneven enforcement including police harassment, racial profiling and greater aggressiveness and use of force when arresting Black people, were common.

Trigger Incident

On the evening of July 12, 1967, near the intersection of 15th Avenue and South 17th Street in Newark, two White police officers pulled over John Smith, a Black cab driver, for a minor traffic violation. The officers alleged that Smith resisted arrest, leading to a physical altercation where Smith was severely beaten by the officers.

News of John Smith's arrest and beating spread quickly through Newark's predominantly Black neighborhoods. Community members, outraged by yet another incident of police brutality, began gathering near the Fourth Precinct police station where Smith was initially taken.

As tensions mounted outside the Fourth Precinct, the police responded with force, deploying tear gas to disperse crowds and control protesters who had gathered. Officers also used the tactic of "baton charges," advancing in formation while wielding batons to forcefully clear areas and restore order.

Police made numerous arrests during the rioting and unrest. There were instances of physical confrontations between officers and protesters, as well as clashes where force was used to subdue individuals resisting arrest or engaging in violent acts. This heavy-handed police response further inflamed the situation, leading to direct clashes between protesters and law enforcement officers.

The Riot

After the initial confrontation near the Fourth Precinct, anger and frustration over long-standing racial discrimination and police brutality boiled over into other neighborhoods of Newark. Mostly-Black mobs spread rapidly across the city.

Escalation. As the riots escalated, there were intense confrontations between mostly-Black protesters and mostly-White law enforcement officers throughout Newark. Police attempted to regain control using tear gas, baton charges and arrests, but the clashes continued amid escalating tensions and sporadic exchanges of gunfire.

Looting and Vandalism. The rioting also caused property damage, with rioters and protesters targeting predominantly White-owned businesses, stores and commercial areas. Widespread looting and vandalism affected shops along Springfield Avenue, Belmont Avenue and other major thoroughfares. Arsonists also targeted several manufacturing plants and warehouses, leading to destruction of property and loss of goods.

Arson attacks by Black rioters were not limited to businesses and industrial sites. Residential buildings in certain areas of Newark, particularly those perceived to be associated with racial tensions or located in areas of heightened unrest, were also set on fire. This included both apartment complexes and single-family homes.

Property Destruction. Public facilities, such as schools, churches and community centers, were not spared from the arson attacks. These institutions, seen as part of the broader systemic issues affecting the Black community in Newark, became targets during the riots, further exacerbating the destruction and chaos.

Troops Deployed. On July 14, 1967, two days after the John Smith arrest, New Jersey Governor Richard J. Hughes deployed approximately 1,500 National Guard troops to assist local law enforcement in restoring order. Governor Hughes requested federal assistance, and on that same day, President Lyndon B. Johnson deployed approximately 3,000 federal troops from the Army's 82nd and 101st Airborne Divisions to assist in restoring order.

The deployment of federal troops sent a strong message that the federal government was taking the situation seriously and was committed to restoring order. This psychological impact helped to reduce the intensity of the unrest and reassure the public.

Army Involvement. Army soldiers patrolled the streets on foot and in armed personnel carriers, enforcing curfews, protecting key locations, including government buildings, businesses and residential areas, and providing a shield against looting, arson and other criminal activities.

The End of the Riot. By July 17, 1967, the combined forces of the National Guard, the Army and law enforcement, coupled with community exhaustion, finally brought an end to the widespread violence.

Immediate Impact

<u>Casualties.</u> The riot had lasted six days, claiming the lives of 26 civilians, mostly Black, and injuring more than 700 (again, mostly Black), including civilians and law enforcement personnel. In all, police arrested and detained over 1,400 people during the unrest.

<u>Property Damage.</u> In addition to the human casualties, the riot caused extensive property damage, estimated at over $10 million (equivalent to around $80 million today). Numerous buildings were looted and burned.

Detroit Riot (July 23-27, 1967)

Background

A second major riot during the "Long Hot Summer" was the Detroit Riot of 1967, also referred to as the Detroit Rebellion. Like Newark, Detroit had a history of racial segregation and discrimination. Despite enactment of the Civil Right Act of 1964, segregation, racial profiling, economic discrimination and other systemic race issues had not improved much since the Riot of 1943 (see previous Chapter).

Trigger Incident

Around 3:30 AM on July 23rd, a team of Detroit Police Department officers executed a raid on the "blind pig" located at 9125 12th Street (now known as Rosa Parks Boulevard). "Blind pig" was a nickname for a bar serving alcohol illegally, usually after hours. In this case, the bar was operating without a liquor license and was known for serving Black patrons.

Police officers arrested several dozen Black people who were inside the bar. According to witness accounts, some of the patrons resisted arrest.

The accumulation of police officers in a residential neighborhood caused tensions to escalate.

The presence of a growing crowd around the bar and the intense police activity sparked anger and frustration among onlookers and residents in the predominantly Black neighborhood. Reports and rumors spread quickly about police brutality and mistreatment during the arrests, fueling community outrage.

The situation escalated into a confrontation between the police and community members who threw stones and bottles at police officers. The unrest quickly spread beyond the immediate area of the bar and by morning, the riots had begun to intensify, with widespread looting, arson and clashes between protesters and law enforcement.

The Riot

Escalation. Over the following days, the riots spread throughout various Detroit neighborhoods. The 12th Street area near the bar saw some of the most intense violence, looting and fires during the early stages of the unrest. Later, rioting spread to the Near West Side adjacent to 12th Street as well as East Side neighborhoods near Gratiot Avenue and Mack Avenue. Eventually, the rioting encompassed the North End and Grand River Avenue as well.

National Guard Deployed. The situation in Detroit quickly escalated beyond the capacity of the local police to handle, prompting Michigan Governor George Romney to deploy approximately 8,000 National Guard troops to restore order on July 23, 1967, the same day the riot began.

Federal Troops. When the Guard deployment proved inadequate to calm the rioting, Governor Romney followed up with a request for federal assistance. Accordingly, on July 25th, U.S President Lyndon B. Johnson authorized the deployment of federal troops, including around

4,700 paratroopers from the 82nd and 101st Airborne Divisions, to take decisive action to quell the violence.

Military Tanks. Federal troops then patrolled the streets with various armored vehicles and tanks with a show of force that played a crucial role in helping to restore order in the city. The first significant use of tanks to defuse rioting in the United States occurred during the 1967 Detroit riots.

Although armored vehicles and tanks had been present in earlier disturbances, their deployment in Detroit marked a notable instance of using such military equipment to manage civil unrest. Canadian folk singer, Gordon Lightfoot, noted the irony of using tanks to calm violence in his 1968 song, "Black Day in July," where he sang "and then the tanks came rolling in to patch things up the best they can."

Underlying Causes

Although triggered by the incident at the blind pig, the riots were a spontaneous and intense expression of frustration and anger over long-standing issues faced by Black residents in Detroit. The actions taken during the riots suggest the Black rioters hoped to end police persecution and violence, attain economic justice, improve living conditions, achieve social and racial equality including educational opportunities and healthcare services, and improve political representation for Black people in government.

It is important to note that many of the rights rioters demanded were already guaranteed to them by federal legislation, such as the Civil Rights Act of 1964.

In the end, the riot resulted in 43 deaths, including 33 Black people and 10 White people. Over 1,100 people were injured, and more than 7,000 people were arrested, making it one of the largest civil disturbances in U.S. history.

Immediate Effect

The riot caused extensive property damage, estimated at over $40 million (equivalent to around $330 million today). Thousands of buildings were destroyed or severely damaged. Leaving large swaths of Black Detroit a desolate wasteland.

The riot also accelerated "White flight" and contributed to the overall economic decline of Detroit.

Kerner Commission. The Kerner Commission's 1968 report highlighted systemic racism, economic inequality and police brutality as root causes of the riots and called for comprehensive reforms.

Conclusion

The Newark and Detroit Riots of 1967 were among the most significant episodes of civil unrest in American history, underscoring the profound racial tensions and systemic inequalities that persisted despite legislative advancements like the Civil Rights Act of 1964. Specific incidents of police brutality triggered these riots, but the fuel for the riots come from a broader context of entrenched racial discrimination, economic disparity and social injustice.

In Newark, long-standing issues such as employment discrimination, redlining, educational inequities and inadequate access to healthcare created a volatile environment. The beating of John Smith by police officers served as the immediate catalyst for the unrest, but the underlying causes were deeply rooted in systemic racism and socio-economic marginalization. The six-day riot resulted in significant loss of life, injuries and extensive property damage, reflecting the community's pent-up frustration and demand for change.

Similarly, the Detroit Riot was precipitated by a single police raid on an unlicensed bar serving Black patrons, but the violence that followed was a response to decades of racial segregation, economic deprivation and discriminatory policing practices. The widespread destruction and loss of life during the five-day riot highlighted the urgent need for addressing the structural inequalities that plagued the city.

The aftermath of both riots saw substantial property damage, economic losses and further racial polarization. The Kerner Commission's 1968 report, which investigated these and other riots, concluded that the nation was "moving toward two societies, one Black, one White— separate and unequal." The report called for comprehensive reforms to address the root causes of racial unrest, including economic and educational opportunities, improved housing, and fair policing practices.

In conclusion, the Newark and Detroit Riots of 1967 were not isolated incidents but part of a larger pattern of racial conflict in America. They underscored the urgent need for systemic change to address the deep-seated issues of racial inequality and injustice that continue to affect American society. The lessons from these riots remain relevant today as the struggle for racial equality and justice continues.

CHAPTER TEN

THE MIAMI RIOT OF 1980

The Miami Riot of 1980, also known as the McDuffie Riot, was a significant episode of civil unrest in Miami, Florida that occurred in May 1980. Following is a comprehensive review of the causes, events and impacts of the riot.

Background

Miami's Black community faced longstanding racial segregation and discrimination. Despite the progress made during the civil rights movement, systemic racism persisted in housing, education and employment.

In 1980, the Black neighborhoods in Miami, particularly Liberty City, were plagued by high unemployment, poverty and inadequate public services. Economic opportunities were limited, leading to widespread frustration and discontent.

The Miami Police Department had a notorious reputation for racial profiling and brutality against Black people, which created deep-seated mistrust and animosity between the Black community and law enforcement.

Trigger Incident

On the night of December 17, 1979, 33-year-old, Arthur McDuffie, a Black man, was riding his Kawasaki motorcycle when he was pursued by police officers for allegedly speeding and running a red light. What ensued was a high-speed chase through the streets of Miami.

The details of the incident that followed remain controversial and were central to the subsequent trial and public outrage. According to the police, McDuffie lost control of his motorcycle and crashed, sustaining fatal injuries as a result. However, later evidence and testimonies revealed a different story.

After McDuffie was apprehended, several male police officers beat him severely with heavy-duty flashlights, nightsticks and their fists. McDuffie suffered multiple skull fractures and was left in a coma. He died four days later, on December 21, 1979.

The officers involved initially attempted to cover up the beating by staging the incident to look like an accident. They reassembled the scene to make it appear as though McDuffie's injuries were the result of a motorcycle crash. Policemen falsified reports and a collaborative effort was made among the officers involved to hide the truth.

Before the end of 1979, four Miami-Dade County police officers were arrested and charged by the Miami-Dade County State Attorney's Office. The charges included manslaughter, evidence tampering and obstruction of justice.

Their trial took place in May 1980. Despite the overwhelming evidence and testimonies about the beating and subsequent cover-up, an all-White jury acquitted the officers of all charges on May 17th.

The Riot

As news of the acquittal spread, residents of Liberty City, a predominantly Black neighborhood in Miami, began to gather spontaneously in the streets. The community had been closely following the case, and the verdict was met with shock, anger and a profound sense of injustice.

Peaceful Protests. The protests started peacefully. Community members came out to express their outrage, chanting slogans, holding signs and calling for justice for Arthur McDuffie. The atmosphere was tense but not immediately violent.

Local leaders and activists attempted to channel the community's anger into organized, peaceful demonstrations. They called for calm and urged protesters to avoid violence and property destruction, hoping to achieve justice through nonviolent means.

Escalation. Despite efforts to maintain peace, the situation quickly became volatile. The crowd's size grew, and emotions ran high. The heavy police presence, including officers in riot gear, further inflamed tensions.

Reports of isolated incidents of vandalism and confrontations between protesters and police began to emerge. Some protesters started throwing rocks and bottles at the police, who responded with force.

Police Response. The situation escalated rapidly when police used tear gas, baton advances, rubber bullets and other crowd-control measures to disperse the increasingly agitated crowd. Protesters perceived this response as another act of aggression by law enforcement.

The initial protests devolved into full-scale riots as night fell. Groups of mostly Black rioters began looting stores, setting fires and attacking both police and civilian targets. The violence spread quickly through Liberty City and into other parts of Miami.

Clashes between rioters and police were intense and brutal. Rioters used Molotov cocktails, and there were reports of gunfire. Police units struggled to contain the chaos.

On May 18, 1980, Florida Governor Bob Graham deployed approximately 2,000 National Guard troops to assist local law enforcement in restoring order. The addition of the Guard to law enforcement personnel, and the efforts of community leaders, proved sufficient to calm hostilities, bringing the riot to an end on May 19, 1980.

Outside Influences. Of the riots covered in this book, The Miami riot was the first to feature substantial outside elements such as agitators, opportunistic criminals and those seeking to exploit the unrest. Rioters from these outside elements (including many White outsiders) engaged in significant looting and vandalism, exacerbating the chaos and destruction in the affected areas. The destruction left large parts of Liberty City in ruins.

The rioting saw mixed reactions from area residents. While many in the community were involved in or supported the protests, others sought to distance themselves from the violence.

Amid the chaos, protestors, both Black and White, continued their calls for justice for McDuffie and broader reforms to address systemic racism and police brutality. Community leaders called for investigations and demanded accountability for the officers involved.

Immediate Impact

Casualties. The riot resulted in 18 deaths, including Black people, White people and Hispanics. No police officers or Guardsmen were reported to be killed. Over 350 people were injured, many of them seriously. Approximately 600 people were arrested during the unrest.

Property Damage. The riot caused extensive property damage, estimated at around $100 million, equivalent to $380 million today. Hundreds of businesses were looted and burned, leaving many blocks of Liberty City and Overtown in ruins.

Long-term Effects

Police Brutality. The Arthur McDuffie incident became a symbol of police brutality and the racial injustices faced by Black people in America. The case highlighted the systemic issues within law enforcement and the judicial system, particularly regarding the treatment of Black people. It also led to calls for police reform and greater accountability for law enforcement officers.

Historical Reference. The 1980 Miami Riot is often referenced in discussions about race relations, police brutality and the need for systemic change within the justice system.

Racial Division. The riot deepened racial divisions in Miami and highlighted the severe economic and social disparities faced by the Black community.

Nationwide Activism. In the riot's aftermath, there was a nationwide surge in community activism aimed at addressing police brutality, economic inequality and improving conditions in Black neighborhoods.

Government Action. The riot prompted Florida's local and state authorities to implement reforms aimed at addressing some of the root causes of the unrest. These included efforts to improve police-community relations and invest in economic development in underserved neighborhoods.

The federal government also became involved, providing funding for community development and social programs aimed at alleviating poverty and improving public services.

Miami Today

Miami is now one of the most ethnically diverse cities in the United States. It has a large Hispanic population, as well as significant Black, Caribbean and other minority communities. Yet systemic racism and entrenched discrimination remain challenging issues.

Income Disparities. Today's Miami has seen some progress since 1980, but significant deficiencies remain. For instance, Miami's White households have a median income of about $103,838, while Black households have a median household income of only $32,212.

Political Representation. There has been an increase in political representation for Black people with applicable elected officials at the local, state and federal level.

Economic Inequity. Significant economic disparities persist. Issues like gentrification and housing affordability remain critical.

Police Reform. While there have been efforts to reform policing practices and improve community relations, instances of police misconduct and racial profiling still occur, leading to ongoing distrust. Racial disparities in arrest and incarceration rates persist, despite reforms aimed at addressing these issues.

Systemic Racism. Systemic issues in education, employment and healthcare continue to affect minority communities disproportionately. Structural barriers prevent equal opportunities and outcomes.

Displacement. Gentrification has displaced many minority communities, particularly in historically Black neighborhoods like Overtown and Liberty City.

Education. Schools in predominantly Black neighborhoods often lack resources compared to those in wealthier, predominantly White areas.

Healthcare. Access to quality healthcare remains unequal, with Black communities facing higher rates of uninsured individuals and poorer health outcomes than White people.

Community Activism. Numerous organizations and community groups are actively working to address these issues through advocacy, policy reform and grassroots initiatives. Examples include:

The Miami Workers Center. The Miami Workers Center was established in 1999 with the mission of empowering low-income communities of color, particularly women, through grassroots organizing, leadership development and advocacy. The center works to build power and achieve systemic change for marginalized communities.

MWC advocates for affordable housing, tenants' rights, and policies to prevent displacement and gentrification. The center works with residents to fight evictions, improve living conditions and ensure access to safe and affordable housing.

The organization supports workers in various industries, focusing on improving labor conditions, securing fair wages and ensuring workers' rights are protected. MWC organizes workers to address issues such as wage theft, workplace safety and discrimination.

MWC has a strong emphasis on empowering women, particularly women of color, through leadership development and advocacy. The center addresses issues such as gender-based violence, reproductive rights and economic inequality.

MWC also encourages civic participation and political engagement among marginalized communities. The center works to increase voter turnout, educate residents on their rights and advocate for policies that promote social and economic justice.

Community Justice Project. CJP provides legal assistance to tenants facing eviction, advocates for affordable housing policies and supports community land trusts to ensure long-term housing stability for low-income residents. The organization works with housing advocates to combat gentrification and displacement, pushing for policies that protect tenants and preserve affordable housing.

CJP advocates for fair labor practices, including the enforcement of wage and hour laws, the protection of workers from exploitation and the promotion of workplace safety.

The organization offers legal support to workers facing discrimination, wage theft and other labor violations, and works to strengthen labor rights for low-wage and immigrant workers.

In addition, CJP addresses environmental racism and advocates for policies that protect low-income communities from environmental hazards. The organization supports campaigns for clean air, water and sustainable development. CJP follows through by providing legal assistance to communities fighting against environmental injustices and harmful development projects.

Finally, CJP conducts workshops, trainings and educational programs to inform communities about their rights and empower them to take action.

Miami-Dade Branch of the NAACP. In addition to providing support similar to the CJP and MWC, the NAACP makes it a priority to advocate for police reform and accountability to address issues of brutality, misconduct and systemic racism within law enforcement.

They work to reform the criminal justice system to ensure fair treatment for all individuals, particularly those from marginalized communities. This includes efforts to end mass incarceration and support for reentry programs.

The organization conducts voter registration drives and educational campaigns to ensure that all eligible voters are informed and able to participate in the electoral process.

The Miami-Dade NAACP also advocates for policies that protect and expand voting rights, fighting against voter suppression and disenfranchisement.

Conclusion

The Miami Riot of 1980 reminds the nation of the deep-seated racial tensions and systemic injustices that have long plagued Miami and other American cities. Triggered by the brutal killing of Arthur McDuffie and the subsequent acquittal of the officers responsible, the riot was not merely a reaction to a singular event, but a manifestation of decades of oppression, economic disenfranchisement and systemic racism faced by Miami's Black community.

The immediate aftermath of the riot saw significant loss of life, widespread injuries and hundreds of millions of dollars in property damage, leaving parts of Liberty City and other neighborhoods in ruins. This violence underscored the profound frustration and anger harbored by the community, which had been pushed to its breaking point by systemic neglect and discrimination.

In the years following the riot, both local and national authorities took steps to address some of the root causes of the unrest. Efforts were made to improve police-community relations, invest in economic development and provide better public services in underserved neighborhoods. Community activism surged, with various organizations advocating for justice, equality and systemic change.

However, despite these efforts and the progress made in some areas, significant challenges remain. Miami today is a city of stark contrasts, where economic disparities and systemic issues continue to disproportionately affect minority communities. Gentrification has displaced many long-standing residents of historically Black neighborhoods, and access to quality education, healthcare and economic opportunities remains unequal.

While Miami is now one of the most ethnically diverse cities in the United States, with increased political representation for Black and other minority communities, the legacy of the 1980 riot is a reminder that the fight for racial justice and equality is far from over. Persistent issues such as police misconduct, racial profiling, and structural barriers in education and employment continue to perpetuate inequality.

Numerous organizations and community groups are actively working to address these issues through advocacy, policy reform and grassroots initiatives. Their efforts are crucial in the ongoing struggle to create a more just and equitable society.

The story of the Miami Riot of 1980 is a powerful testament to the enduring resilience and determination of the Black community in Miami. It serves as both a cautionary tale and a call to action, highlighting the necessity of continued vigilance and effort to combat systemic racism and ensure that all citizens have the opportunity to thrive.

CHAPTER ELEVEN
LOS ANGELES RIOTS OF 1992

The Los Angeles Riots of 1992, also known as the Rodney King Riots or the LA Uprising, were a series of widespread civil disturbances that occurred in Los Angeles, California following the acquittal of four police officers involved in the beating of Rodney King, a Black man. The riots lasted for six days, from April 29 to May 4, 1992, and in addition to injuries and deaths, resulted in the greatest property damage caused by any riot in U.S. history. Following is a detailed overview of the causes, key incidents and aftermath of the riots.

Background

In 1992, Los Angeles had a long history of racial tension and discrimination, particularly between the Black community and the Los Angeles Police Department (LAPD). Economic disparities and social inequalities were also prevalent, with many Black people living in impoverished neighborhoods with limited opportunities.

The LAPD had a notorious reputation for excessive force and racial profiling, particularly against Black people and other minority groups. Incidents of police brutality were often overlooked or dismissed by law enforcement and the judicial system.

Trigger Incident

On March 3, 1991, Rodney King, a 25-year-old Black motorist, was pulled over by LAPD officers after a high-speed chase. The pursuit began when King, who was driving under the influence, refused to pull over, leading officers on a pursuit that reached speeds of up to 115 miles per hour.

Video Evidence of Beating. After King finally stopped, he was forcibly removed from his vehicle and subjected to a brutal beating by four LAPD officers. The beating was captured on videotape by a bystander who witnessed the incident from his apartment balcony.

The video footage showed officers repeatedly striking King with batons and kicking him, even after he was lying on the ground and appeared to pose no threat.

Indictment. Following widespread public outrage over the beating, on April 17, 1991, a Los Angeles grand jury indicted the four LAPD officers charging them with assault with a deadly weapon and use of excessive force under color of authority.

Change of Venue. The venue for the trial was moved to Simi Valley due to concerns over pretrial publicity and the potential for bias in Los Angeles County. The move was intended to ensure a fair trial and to minimize the influence of local sentiment and public opinion that might have prejudiced jurors against the defendants.

The choice of Simi Valley as the trial venue became controversial, as critics argued that it resulted in a jury that was less representative of the diversity and viewpoints present in Los Angeles County, where the incident had occurred. The venue decision played a significant role in shaping the outcome of the trial and its subsequent impact on public perception and civil unrest.

BLACK DAYS
Page 145

The Trial. The trial itself began on February 25, 1992, and lasted for several weeks. Prosecutors argued that the officers used excessive force against Rodney King, who was unarmed and lying on the ground during the beating captured on video. The defense contended that the officers' actions were justified given the circumstances of King's resistance and the need to subdue him.

The jury for the trial was composed of ten White jurors, one Hispanic juror and one biracial juror. There were no Black jurors on the panel.

Acquittal. On April 29, 1992, the jury acquitted all four officers of assault charges and acquitted three of them of using excessive force.

The Riots

The acquittal of the officers sparked immediate outrage in Los Angeles. Within hours, protests erupted in South Central Los Angeles, where much of the city's Black population resided.

Over the next six days, the riots spread to other parts of Los Angeles and neighboring cities, including Koreatown and Hollywood. Predominantly Black rioters targeted businesses, particularly those owned by White people, Koreans and other ethnic minorities.

Escalation. It didn't take long before various local groups with widely disparate agendas joined the rioting. Taking advantage of the chaos, street gangs such as the Bloods, Crips and others, participated in looting, arson and violence.

Outside Elements. Other outside agitators, including anarchists and anti-police activists, saw the unrest as an opportunity to protest against various perceived injustices and systemic issues. They joined in as well, often contributing additional violence to the mix.

Looting. Many young people, both from local neighborhoods and outside, were involved in looting and vandalism contributing to the overall disorder and violence.

Police Deployment. The LAPD deployed an estimated 6,000 to 7,000 officers to riot control duty. The Los Angeles County Sheriff's Department mobilized an additional 2,000 to 3,000 of its deputies to help.

National Guard Deployment. On April 30th, the second day of rioting, California Governor Pete Wilson ordered the deployment of approximately 10,000 California National Guard troops to assist in restoring order and controlling the unrest. This deployment marked one of the largest domestic uses of the National Guard in response to civil unrest in U.S. history.

Federal Assistance. Governor Wilson also requested federal help, but specifically in the form of federal law enforcement agencies and resources, not federal troops. President George H.W. Bush responded by mobilizing federal law enforcement agencies, including the FBI, ATF (Bureau of Alcohol, Tobacco, Firearms and Explosives) and U.S. Marshals Service, to support local authorities in controlling the situation. Additionally, federal assets such as aircraft were used for surveillance and logistical support during the unrest.

The Guard troops and additional federal law enforcement personnel began arriving in Los Angeles on the evening of April 30, 1992, and their deployment continued into the following days. The Guard performed its usual duties of patrolling the streets, protecting critical infrastructure and enforcing curfews. Armored vehicles such as personnel carriers were deployed for defensive purposes, such as creating barriers, securing areas to prevent further damage and to protect law enforcement personnel and civilians.

Police Tactics. Law enforcement deployed tear gas to disperse crowds and deter rioters and shot rubber bullets and bean bag rounds to discourage rioters. They used pepper spray to temporarily incapacitate individuals and water cannons to disperse crowds. On occasion, police used flashbang grenades to disorient and distract rioters.

Police officers also employed crowd control techniques such as forming lines, creating barriers and issuing verbal commands to direct crowds and prevent escalation of violence.

Federal Role. The role of the federal agents was mainly to provide advanced technology, logistical support and tactical advice to LAPD.

Rioting Ends. In the end, it took interventions by community leaders, activist groups and local clergy, as well as pressure from extensive nationwide media coverage, to finally end the violence on May 4th, 1992.

Immediate Impact

Casualties and Damage. The riots resulted in 63 deaths—50 to 60 Black people and less than 10 White people—over 2,000 injuries and more than 12,000 arrests. Property damage was estimated at $800 million to over $1 billion (approximately $1.8 billion to 2.2 billion in 2024 dollars). Thousands of buildings including homes and businesses were looted, burned or destroyed.

Racial Tensions. The riots exacerbated racial tensions and deepened divisions within the city. Many Black and minority-owned businesses were destroyed, further exacerbating economic hardships in already marginalized communities.

National Scrutiny. The riots also brought renewed national attention to issues of police brutality, racial injustice and economic inequality, prompting calls for reform within the LAPD and leading to changes in law enforcement policies and practices across the country.

Civil Rights Charges. The U.S. Attorney General's Office brought charges against the four acquitted officers for violating Rodney King's civil rights. In April 1993, two of the officers were convicted and sentenced to 2.5 years in federal prison.

Long-term Effects

Following the 1992 LA riots, America experienced a notable shift in public opinion and political mobilization around issues of social justice and inequality.

Increased Awareness of Racial Injustice. The riots brought national attention to issues of police brutality, racial discrimination and socioeconomic disparities, particularly in urban areas. The graphic images and media coverage of the riots highlighted the frustrations and grievances of minority communities.

Political Response and Policy Changes. The riots prompted political leaders and policymakers to address systemic issues affecting marginalized communities. There was renewed focus on implementing reforms in policing practices, enhancing community relations and investing in economic development in underserved neighborhoods.

Community Empowerment and Activism. The riots galvanized community activism and grassroots movements aimed at advocating for civil rights and social justice. Organizations like the NAACP, ACLU and others intensified their efforts to push for legislative changes and hold accountable those responsible for injustices.

Impact on Public Discourse. Discussions on race relations, inequality and the role of government in addressing social issues became more prominent in public discourse. Media outlets, scholars and intellectuals analyzed the root causes of the riots and proposed solutions to prevent similar unrest in the future.

Long-Term Policy Reforms. Over time, the riots contributed to ongoing efforts to reform criminal justice policies, promote diversity and inclusion and dismantle systemic racism. Initiatives focused on community policing, diversity training for law enforcement, and equitable access to resources gained momentum in various cities.

Economic Effects. The riots caused extensive damage to businesses and infrastructure in predominantly minority neighborhoods, exacerbating economic disparities and contributing to an already-acute deficiency of capital investments in Black communities.

Police Relations. Trust between communities of color and law enforcement was severely strained, prompting efforts to improve community policing and build trust through outreach and reform initiatives.

Civil Right Act Enforcement. The federal civil rights trial of the LA Police officers marked a new avenue of federal intervention in a case of alleged police brutality. The trial set a legal precedent in the application of federal civil rights laws to cases involving police misconduct. And it underscored the federal government's role in addressing civil rights violations, particularly when state prosecutions may have resulted in acquittals or insufficient accountability.

The Civil Rights trial also carried significant symbolic importance in the context of race relations and police-community relations in the United States. And although the 30-month prison terms handed out at the trial were seen by some as relatively lenient, the fact that there was a conviction at all represented progress to many.

Los Angeles Today

Today in Los Angeles, a disparity in income still exists between Black people and White people, with median White household income at

$97,663 and only $51,940 for median Black households. And several other areas remain in need of attention.

Policing and Criminal Justice. Still today, LA has ongoing problems with racial profiling, excessive use of force and disparities in treatment within the criminal justice system. Black individuals are disproportionately stopped, arrested and incarcerated compared to their White counterparts.

Initiatives for police reform, such as community policing and de-escalation training, continue to be implemented, but challenges remain in achieving equitable outcomes.

Economic Inequality. Black communities in Los Angeles face higher rates of unemployment, lower incomes and limited access to economic opportunities compared to White residents. Historical redlining practices continue to impact wealth accumulation and economic mobility.

Education. Educational disparities also persist, with Black students experiencing higher dropout rates, lower academic achievement and disparities in access to quality education compared to their White peers.

Healthcare. Black communities in LA continue to experience higher rates of chronic diseases, limited access to preventive care and healthcare discrimination.

Housing and Neighborhood Disparities. Residential segregation continues to impact Black communities, leading to disparities in housing quality, affordability and neighborhood resources. Gentrification and housing discrimination contribute to displacement and exacerbate housing instability in some neighborhoods.

Private Organizations. In the wake of the Rodney King riots, Los Angeles has seen the creation or significant expansion of a number of organizations and initiatives to combat racial injustices. Examples include:

Black Lives Matter Los Angeles (BLM LA). Founded in 2013, BLM LA seeks to eradicate white supremacy and build local power to intervene in violence inflicted on Black communities by the state and vigilantes. Its activities include organizing protests, policy advocacy, community engagement and public education campaigns.

California Black Women's Health Project (CABWHP). Founded in 1994, the California Black Women's Health Project has the mission of improving the health and wellness of Black women and girls in California through advocacy, education, outreach and policy development. It programs include: health education, advocacy training, and community engagement initiatives focused on mental health, reproductive health and overall wellness.

Dignity and Power Now. Established in 2012, the mission of Dignity and Power Now I to fight for the dignity and power of incarcerated people, their families and communities. It supports campaigns for civilian oversight of jails, mental health diversion programs and ending law enforcement violence.

JusticeLA. Founded in 2017, JusticeLA seeks to reduce the footprint of incarceration in Los Angeles County and reinvest dollars into community-based systems of care. Among its activities are advocacy for criminal justice reform, community organizing and policy change to reduce incarceration rates and improve community services.

Community Coalition. The coalition was founded in 1990, but its role expanded significantly post-King riots. Its mission is to help transform the social and economic conditions in South Los Angeles that foster addiction, crime, violence and poverty by building a community institution that involves thousands of LA residents in creating, influencing and changing public policy.

Los Angeles Black Worker Center (LABWC). Established in 2011, the Worker Center seeks to build power among Black workers and the extended community to expand access to quality jobs, address workplace discrimination and transform industries. Its work includes workforce development, policy advocacy, leadership training and organizing in support of fair labor practices.

Youth Justice Coalition (YJC). Founded in the early 2000s, the YJC's mission is to build a youth-led movement to challenge race, gender and class inequality in Los Angeles County's and California's juvenile justice systems. It provides policy advocacy, leadership development and community organizing to reform the juvenile justice system and support youth of color.

Anti-Recidivism Coalition (ARC). Established in 2013, the ARC aims to end mass incarceration in California and empower formerly incarcerated individuals to live better lives. Its activities include advocacy, mentoring, job training and providing support for reentry to society.

Justice Warriors for Black Lives. Founded Post-2015, Justice Warriors for Black Lives advocates for the rights and well-being of Black individuals, particularly focusing on issues of police brutality and systemic racism. Its activities include organizing protests, community events and policy advocacy.

Conclusion

The Los Angeles Riots of 1992, sparked by the acquittal of four LAPD officers in the beating of Rodney King, stand as a pivotal moment in American history, exposing deep-seated issues of racial injustice, economic disparity and systemic discrimination. Lasting six days, these riots resulted in loss of life, property damage of unparalleled proportions and heightened tensions across the city.

In the aftermath, Los Angeles and the nation underwent a period of reflection and reform. The riots catalyzed a surge in public awareness and political mobilization around issues of police brutality, social equity and civil rights. Advocacy groups intensified efforts to hold institutions accountable for misconduct, while policymakers sought to implement reforms in law enforcement, education, healthcare and economic development.

Despite these efforts, the racial disparities at the heart of the riots endure in Los Angeles today. Disparities persist in income, policing practices, educational opportunities, healthcare access and housing equity, disproportionately affecting Black communities. Ongoing initiatives aim to address these inequities, yet significant challenges remain in achieving true equality and justice for all Angelenos.

The events of 1992 underscore the resilience of communities in the face of adversity and the ongoing imperative to confront systemic racism and promote inclusive policies. As Los Angeles continues its journey toward healing and equity, the lessons of the Rodney King Riots serve as a powerful reminder of the need for continued vigilance, dialogue and action in pursuit of a more just and equitable society.

CHAPTER TWELVE

THE FERGUSON UNREST OF 2014

The Ferguson Unrest of 2014 refers to the civil unrest and protests that erupted in Ferguson, Missouri following the fatal shooting of Michael Brown, an unarmed Black teenager, by a White police officer on August 9, 2014. The shooting and subsequent events ignited a national debate on issues of race, policing and social justice in the United States. Following is a detailed overview of the causes, key incidents and aftermath of the unrest.

Background

In 2014, the predominantly Black community of Ferguson, Missouri, became a focal point of national attention due to the shooting of Michael Brown, an unarmed Black teenager, by a White police officer. The incident and its aftermath highlighted systemic racism and longstanding issues within the city, including:

<u>Policing Practices.</u> Ferguson's police department had a history of disproportionately targeting Black residents through practices such as racial profiling, excessive force and discriminatory traffic stops. Although, two-thirds of the city's residents were Black people, statistics indicate that 86% of all traffic stops accrued to Black drivers.

Justice System Disparities. The judicial system in Ferguson exhibited racial disparities, where Black individuals were more likely to be arrested, charged with offenses and face harsher penalties compared to their White counterparts for similar offenses. This disparity extended to the municipal court system, where Black people were disproportionately fined and subjected to fees, contributing to cycles of poverty and legal entanglement.

Economic Inequality. Ferguson exhibited stark economic disparities along racial lines. Black residents faced higher rates of unemployment, lower wages and limited access to economic opportunities compared to White residents. Historical practices like redlining had restricted Black homeownership and access to financial resources, perpetuating economic inequities and housing disparities.

Political Representation. Despite Ferguson having a predominantly Black population, the city's political representation did not reflect this demographic reality. The majority-White local elected representatives failed to advocate to the satisfaction of the Black residents.

Social Segregation. Residential segregation persisted in Ferguson, with distinct racial divisions in housing patterns and neighborhood development. This segregation contributed to disparities in access to quality education, healthcare services and community resources, further perpetuating socioeconomic inequalities.

Community Relations with Law Enforcement. Tensions between the Ferguson Police Department and the Black community were longstanding, marked by mistrust and perceptions of racial bias.

Trigger Incident

On August 9, 2014, Michael Brown, an 18-year-old Black man, was shot and killed by Ferguson police officer, Darren Wilson. Brown was unarmed at the time of the shooting.

The incident began when the officer Wilson encountered Michael Brown and a friend, Dorian Johnson, walking down the middle of the street. According to witnesses, an altercation ensued between Brown and Wilson, which led to Wilson firing his weapon, striking Brown multiple times. Eyewitness details of the incident vary widely.

After Michael Brown was shot, his body remained on the street for several hours, which drew criticism and intensified community anger due to what was perceived as a lack of respect and urgency in handling the situation.

Ferguson Police officers quickly responded to the scene, leading to an immediate confrontation with residents who were gathering to witness and protest the shooting.

The Unrest

The shooting of Michael Brown sparked widespread protests and civil unrest in Ferguson, with demonstrators demanding justice for Brown and addressing broader issues of police brutality and racial discrimination. A brief timeline of the unrest follows:

August 10, 2014. Residents of Ferguson, both Black and White, organize a peaceful vigil to honor Michael Brown's memory. The event draws a crowd of hundreds and calls for justice begin to escalate.

August 11, 2014. The first night of protests turns confrontational as demonstrators clash with police officers near the site of the shooting. Police deploy tear gas to disperse the crowd.

August 12, 2014. Protests intensify, spreading to other parts of Ferguson. Some demonstrators engage in looting, vandalism and arson, leading to property damage and arrests.

August 13-14, 2014. Law enforcement agencies, including the Ferguson Police Department and the Missouri State Highway Patrol, respond with a heavily militarized presence. Armored vehicles and riot gear are used to control crowds.

August 15, 2014. Missouri Governor Jay Nixon declares a state of emergency and imposes a curfew in Ferguson from midnight to 5 a.m. in an attempt to restore order and prevent further violence.

August 16-17, 2014. Despite the curfew, tensions remain high, with sporadic clashes between protesters and police. Some community leaders and activists criticize the curfew as exacerbating rather than calming the situation.

August 18, 2014. Missouri Governor Jay Nixon deploys approximately 700 National Guard troops to Ferguson to assist law enforcement in maintaining security and protecting public safety.

Also, by this date, agitators with varying agendas join local protestors, leading to increasing chaos.

August 19-20, 2014. Amid ongoing protests and unrest, community leaders, clergy members and activists engage in dialogue with local authorities and residents to seek ways to de-escalate tensions and address grievances.

August 21-25, 2014. The presence of the National Guard and community-led efforts gradually helped to calm the situation in Ferguson. Nightly protests continue, but with reduced intensity compared to earlier days. [End timeline]

Immediate Impact

The Ferguson Unrest left a lasting impact on the city of Ferguson, leading to significant changes in local governance, law enforcement practices and community engagement.

Hands Up; Don't Shoot. Multiple witnesses claimed to have seen Brown with his hands raised in the air when he was shot by Officer Wilson, although these accounts varied and were disputed during the subsequent investigations. The phrase "hands up; don't shoot" quickly became a rallying cry for protesters who took to the streets in Ferguson and across the country to demand justice for Michael Brown and to call attention to police violence against Black individuals.

Casualties. There were no reports of fatalities during the unrest, although several injuries occurred among both protesters and law enforcement officers due to clashes, use of tear gas and other confrontations. The lack of deaths resulting from the protests presented a marked departure from many previous occasions of civil unrest.

Property Damage. At points, the unrest included incidents of looting, arson, vandalism and confrontations with police. Property damage has been estimated at "tens of millions of dollars," meaning that the Ferguson Unrest was of a different character (less destructive) from some other fiercely violent confrontations detailed in this book.

Outside Elements. It is difficult to assess the extent to which outside agitators caused property damage or injury. But it is believed they had a material impact.

Grand Jury. Shortly after the shooting in August, the St. Louis County Prosecuting Attorney's Office convened a grand jury to consider the possibility of bringing charges against Officer Wilson. The prosecution's approach to presenting charges to the grand jury in the case of the shooting was met with significant scrutiny and controversy.

It is worth understanding how that process worked and how it *should* have worked.

Grand juries are typically used to decide whether there is enough evidence to charge accused persons with a crime and then to proceed with a criminal trial. Therefore, the prosecuting attorney usually brings forth all of the evidence in favor of conviction without allowing the jury to hear evidence that might imply innocence.

In this case, prosecutors presented evidence which was characterized as "a comprehensive overview of the circumstances surrounding the incident." Evidence supporting a decision to indict the accused, as well as evidence to support dismissal of charges (exculpatory evidence), was all introduced to the grand jury.

On November 24, 2014, the grand jury announced its decision not to indict Officer Darren Wilson, sparking immediate and widespread protests in Ferguson and around the country.

The handling of the grand jury proceedings drew criticism from various quarters. Critics argued that prosecutors had not presented the case in a manner that sufficiently advocated for charges against Officer Wilson.

The Department of Justice (DOJ) conducted a separate investigation into the shooting and the Ferguson Police Department's practices. In March 2015, the DOJ issued its report finding that that there was "insufficient evidence to support federal criminal civil rights charges against Officer Darren Wilson."

However, the DOJ also issued a report highlighting systemic issues within the Ferguson Police Department and the municipal court system, including patterns of racial bias and unconstitutional policing practices. This report included a scathing criticism of the systemic racial bias within the Ferguson Police Department and municipal court system.

Long-term Effects

Consent Decree. In 2016, the city of Ferguson entered into a consent decree with the U.S. Department of Justice. The decree mandated comprehensive reforms in the police department and municipal court system. These reforms were designed to address the patterns of racial bias and unconstitutional police and court practices identified by the DOJ's investigation.

Political Changes. In June 2020, Ferguson elected its first Black mayor, Ella Jones. Jones' platform emphasized the need for unity and reform. The composition of the Ferguson City Council became more diverse, with an increased constituency of Black members.

Efforts were made to increase community engagement in local governance. Town hall meetings, community forums and other participatory events became more common, providing residents with more opportunities to voice their concerns and influence policy decisions.

Police Reforms. The Ferguson Police Department implemented several reforms recommended by the DOJ, including changes in use-of-force policies, increased training on racial bias and de-escalation techniques and the adoption of body-worn cameras by police officers to increase transparency and accountability.

There was a shift towards community policing strategies, which emphasized building relationships between law enforcement officers and the communities they serve. This approach aimed to improve trust and cooperation between the police and residents.

Activism. The unrest galvanized grassroots activism and the formation of local organizations focused on social justice, police accountability and community empowerment. Groups like the Ferguson Action

Committee emerged to advocate for systemic change and to monitor the implementation of reforms.

Youth Engagement. Young people in Ferguson became more politically active and engaged in advocacy work. Programs and initiatives were developed to empower youth and encourage their participation in civic activities and community leadership.

Economic Initiatives. Efforts were made by government and private institutions to address the economic disparities that had contributed to the unrest. Efforts such as the Ferguson 1000 jobs initiative and the Ferguson Forward initiative by local businesses to offer job training and career development services to Black people were launched to create more opportunities for residents.

Black Lives Matter. The unrest in Ferguson galvanized a national movement for racial justice and police reform, inspiring activists and organizations to mobilize against police brutality and advocate for systemic change. The Black Lives Matter movement in particular gained momentum in the wake of the Ferguson protests.

Ferguson Today

Income Disparities. In 2024, racial disparities in median household income persisted, with the median White household receiving $56,266 and its Black counterpart receiving only $38,658.

Systemic Racism. Systemic racism against Black people in Ferguson remains a problem. While there have been improvements and reforms, challenges remain in several key areas, including policing, economic opportunities, education and housing.

Racial Profiling. Black residents of Ferguson still report experiencing racial profiling and discriminatory treatment by law enforcement. Data often shows that Black individuals are disproportionately stopped, searched and arrested compared to their White counterparts.

Consent Decree Effects. The consent decree with the Department of Justice (DOJ) has led to some improvements in police practices and oversight, but full compliance and cultural change within the police department have been slow.

Trust between the Black community and the police remains strained. Incidents of excessive force and perceived injustice continue to impact community-police relations.

Efforts such as community policing and the establishment of a citizen review board are ongoing but have not fully bridged the trust gap.

Economic Disparities. Black residents in Ferguson face higher rates of unemployment and underemployment compared to White residents. Economic opportunities remain limited, particularly in the most marginalized neighborhoods.

Job training and economic development initiatives have been implemented, but systemic barriers to employment, such as discrimination and lack of access to quality education, persist.

Education. Black students in Ferguson continue to face disparities in educational outcomes, including lower graduation rates and standardized test scores compared to their White peers.

Schools in predominantly Black neighborhoods often have fewer resources, experienced teachers and advanced educational programs, contributing to the achievement gap.

Discriminatory school discipline practices disproportionately affect Black students, leading to higher suspension and expulsion rates and contributing to the school-to-prison pipeline.

Environmental Racism. Black communities face greater environmental hazards, such as exposure to pollution and inadequate infrastructure, which can negatively impact health and quality of life.

Political Representation. Although there have been improvements in political representation, including the election of Black officials, disparities remain in the political influence and power held by Black residents.

Efforts to increase voter registration and participation among Black residents are ongoing, aiming to ensure their voices are heard in local governance.

Activism. Grassroots organizations and community activists continue to play a vital role in advocating for social justice and equity in Ferguson. These groups work to address systemic racism and support community-led initiatives for change.

Conclusion

The Ferguson Unrest of 2014 marked a pivotal moment in the national conversation about race, policing and social justice in the United States. The fatal shooting of Michael Brown and the subsequent protests and civil unrest exposed deep-seated issues within Ferguson and similar communities across the country. The systemic racism that permeated various aspects of life in Ferguson—policing practices, the justice system, economic inequality, political representation, and social segregation—came to the forefront, demanding urgent attention and action.

The immediate impact of the unrest led to significant changes in Ferguson's local governance, law enforcement practices and community engagement. The election of the city's first Black mayor, the diversification of the city council and the implementation of DOJ-mandated reforms in the police department and municipal court system represented steps toward addressing long-standing racial biases and building a more inclusive community.

Economic initiatives aimed at reducing disparities, such as job training and development programs, were launched to create more opportunities for residents. Community policing strategies were emphasized to rebuild trust between law enforcement and the community. Grassroots activism and local organizations emerged to advocate for continued reform and accountability, reflecting the ongoing commitment to achieving social justice.

Despite these efforts, the challenges of systemic racism remain. Black residents of Ferguson still face higher rates of unemployment, economic inequality and educational disparities. The legacy of residential segregation and discriminatory practices continues to affect access to quality housing, education and healthcare. Trust between the Black community and the police, although improving, remains fragile, highlighting the need for sustained efforts in community engagement and reform.

The long-term effects of the Ferguson unrest extend beyond the city itself, having galvanized a national movement for racial justice and police reform. The Black Lives Matter movement in particular gained momentum in the wake of the Ferguson protests, advocating for an end to police brutality and systemic racism across the nation.

In conclusion, while Ferguson has made notable progress since 2014, the path to true equity and justice is ongoing. The city serves as a microcosm of broader national issues, reminding us of the importance of continued vigilance, activism and reform to dismantle systemic racism and create a more just society for all.

CHAPTER THIRTEEN

THE BALTIMORE PROTESTS OF 2015

The Baltimore protests of 2015, also known as the Baltimore Uprising, were a series of civil disturbances and demonstrations that occurred in Baltimore, Maryland, following the death of Freddie Gray, a 25-year-old Black man who sustained fatal injuries while in police custody. The protests, which lasted for several days, brought national attention to issues of police brutality, racial injustice and socioeconomic inequality once again. Following is a detailed overview of the causes, key incidents and aftermath of the protests.

Background

In April 2015, Baltimore, like many other American cities, was characterized by systemic racism deeply rooted in its social, economic and political fabric. The city's history of racial inequality can be traced back to various policies and practices that disadvantaged Black residents over decades.

In the early 20th century, Baltimore was one of the first cities to adopt racially discriminative zoning laws. Although such laws were eventually deemed unconstitutional, discriminatory practices continued through redlining which led to disinvestment, lower property values and segregation that persisted for decades.

Urban renewal projects across Baltimore in the mid-20th century also demonstrated discriminatory effects, collectively displacing an estimated 25,000 to 30,000 people, with a significant proportion being Black residents.

Charles Center and Inner Harbor Projects. For example, in the 1950s and 1960s, Baltimore launched major urban renewal initiatives, including the Charles Center and Inner Harbor redevelopment projects. These projects aimed to revitalize the downtown area but had the effect of displacing of Black communities because urban authorities deemed these neighborhoods "blighted" or "unsafe." The construction of these commercial and tourist areas led to the demolition of homes and businesses in predominantly Black neighborhoods without adequate compensation or relocation assistance.

Highway to Nowhere. Another example is the proposed I-170 project, later dubbed the "Highway to Nowhere," which was intended to connect I-70 to downtown Baltimore, passing through predominantly Black neighborhoods like Harlem Park and Rosemont.

Construction activities on this project alone demolished approximately 971 homes and 62 businesses, displacing around 1,500 residents, many of whom were Black. Compensation for the losses and for relocation expenses was grossly inadequate.

Due to political pressure, the city ultimately halted the project in the late 1970s. The highway ended abruptly, hence the moniker "Highway to Nowhere." But despite never being completed, the project's damage had already been done. Cleared land and partially built highway structures created physical and psychological barriers in the community, further contributing to neighborhood decline and disinvestment.

Additionally, the loss of homes and businesses disrupted tightly knit communities, breaking up social networks and community support systems. The affected neighborhoods saw a decline in property values (resulting in inadequate school funding) and an increase in vacant lots (contributing to blight and further disinvestment).

Public Housing Demolition. The demolition of public housing projects, such as Murphy Homes and Lexington Terrace in the 1990s under the HOPE VI program, aimed to reduce concentrated poverty. However, these efforts also led to the displacement of predominantly Black residents without adequate replacement housing or support. Although residents received Section 8 vouchers, many struggled to find affordable housing in safer, more integrated neighborhoods, perpetuating the cycle of segregation and economic hardship.

Employment Discrimination. Black people in Baltimore faced discriminatory hiring practices and a lack of access to quality education and training programs. The decline of industrial jobs in the latter half of the 20th century particularly affected Black workers, leading to higher unemployment rates and economic instability in their communities.

Racial Profiling and Over-Policing. Black communities in Baltimore experienced aggressive policing strategies. Policies such as "zero-tolerance" policing disproportionately targeted Black people, leading to higher arrest rates and incarceration.

The relationship between the police and Black residents was strained due to frequent instances of racial profiling, harassment and excessive use of force. Many Black residents reported frequent stops by police officers that were seemingly without cause.

During stops, police officers often conducted invasive searches without proper cause or consent. This included pat-downs and vehicle searches that were seen as humiliating and degrading, as well as unnecessary force or abuse of detainees.

Tyrone West. One example is the case of Tyrone West, a 44-year-old Black man who died in 2013 after being restrained and repeatedly struck by police officers during a traffic stop. Witnesses reported excessive force, and the incident highlighted concerns about police brutality. The Medical Examiner reported the official cause of death as cardiac arrhythmia, exacerbated by dehydration and the stress of the physical altercation with police. The report did not definitively attribute the death to police actions alone.

Despite the controversy and calls for justice, no criminal charges were ever brought against the officers involved in Tyrone West's death. The decision not to prosecute was based on the medical examiner's findings and the determination that there was insufficient evidence to prove criminal conduct beyond a reasonable doubt.

Justice Inequities. After arrest, Black people faced harsher sentencing and were more likely to be incarcerated for minor offenses compared to their White counterparts.

Access to Healthcare. Black people in Baltimore had less access to quality healthcare facilities and services and higher rates of chronic illnesses, such as diabetes and hypertension as a result.

Environmental Racism. Black residents often lived in neighborhoods that were located in areas with higher exposure to environmental hazards, such as industrial pollution and lead contamination, further impacting residents' health.

Voter Suppression and Political Marginalization. Historical voter suppression tactics and ongoing political marginalization limited Black participation in local governance and policymaking. The dearth of political representation and voting clout hindered activist's efforts to address systemic racism and inequality.

Trigger Incident

On the morning of April 12, 2015, Freddie Carlos Gray Jr., a 25-year-old Black man, was arrested by Baltimore police officers after fleeing upon making eye contact with one of them. The officers were patrolling a high-crime area known for drug activity.

According to the police, Gray was found carrying a switchblade (later determined to be a legal folding knife). There were no other illegal items in Gray's possession. He was apprehended at 8:40 a.m. in the Sandtown-Winchester neighborhood.

Gray was placed in a police van, handcuffed and later shackled, but not secured with a seatbelt—a violation of police policy. Video footage captured by a bystander shows Gray being dragged into a police van, visibly in pain and unable to walk on his own. The van made several stops on the way to the police station, during which Gray's condition deteriorated.

During one stop, Gray was taken out of the van, placed in leg irons, and reloaded, but still not secured with a seatbelt.

During the ride, Gray sustained a severe spinal cord injury. Accordingly, Gray arrived at the Western District police station unresponsive. He was immediately taken to the trauma center at the University of Maryland Medical Center, where reports indicate that by that time, he had fallen into a coma. He had sustained a broken neck, and his spinal cord was 80% severed at the C4 and C5 vertebrae.

Gray underwent surgery but remained in a coma. He died a week later, on April 19, 2015, from complications due to his spinal injury.

The Protests

Peaceful Protests. Almost immediately after Freddie Gray's death, residents and civil rights groups led peaceful protests and vigils to demand answers and seek justice for Gray and his family. However, tensions increased after Gray's funeral on April 27, 2015.

Escalation. On the afternoon of April 27, protests in Baltimore turned violent, with clashes between demonstrators and police. Rioting, looting and arson erupted in several neighborhoods, particularly in West Baltimore.

National Guard Deployed. That same day, Maryland Governor Larry Hogan declared a state of emergency in Baltimore and deployed approximately 2,000 National Guard troops to help restore order. That number later grew to over 3,000.

Federal Assistance. Governor Hogan also requested federal assistance and on April 27th, U.S. President Barack Obama directed the sending of increased support from federal law enforcement agencies rather than the deployment of federal troops.

The Department of Justice, the Federal Bureau of Investigation (FBI) and the Bureau of Alcohol, Tobacco, Firearms and Explosives (ATF) provided resources, intelligence and personnel to assist local and state law enforcement efforts.

Mondawmin Mall. Demonstrations turned confrontational near Mondawmin Mall in Northwest Baltimore. A mob of racially diverse rioters vandalized police vehicles, set fires to buildings and cars and looted several businesses. Pharmacies, liquor stores and convenience stores presented convenient targets.

Violence Spreads. In the following days, the unrest spread to other parts of Baltimore, including downtown areas and neighborhoods like Penn

North and West Baltimore. Mondawmin Mall was closed early due to safety concerns as the situation escalated.

Leaders Seek Peace. Community leaders and residents attempted to intervene and prevent further violence. There were also efforts by clergy and local activists to de-escalate tensions.

Amid the chaos, news crews also reported instances of community members coming together to clean up debris and support local businesses affected by the unrest, highlighting the resilience and solidarity of Baltimore residents.

Arson. Multiple fires were reported throughout the city, straining emergency services as they responded to fires, medical emergencies and incidents of violence simultaneously.

Outside Elements. Law enforcement officials and community leaders in Baltimore expressed concerns that some of the violence and property destruction during the unrest were instigated or exacerbated by individuals from outside the local community.

These "outside agitators" were believed to have traveled to Baltimore specifically to participate in or escalate the protests, using the situation as an opportunity to pursue their several and diverse agendas through increased chaos. Some were simply criminals who were there to loot. Others were there to incite violent confrontations with police.

The presence of outside agitators became a topic of discussion in media coverage and public discourse about the unrest. It shaped varying perceptions about the nature and causes of the violence, with some focusing on external influences rather than underlying local grievances.

Immediate Impact

Casualties. In addition to Freddie Gray, reports indicate that there were other fatalities during the unrest, but the exact number and circumstances of these deaths vary in different accounts.

Some fatalities were attributed to unrelated violence or medical emergencies that occurred amid the unrest, but comprehensive official records specifying the total number of deaths directly related to the events have not been made public.

Property Damage. Property damage from the unrest in Baltimore totaled in the millions of dollars. Exact figures vary, but initial estimates suggested that hundreds of businesses were damaged, looted or destroyed by fire during the riots. The damage affected both small businesses and larger commercial establishments in multiple neighborhoods across the city.

In addition to businesses, public infrastructure such as vehicles, streetlights and public buildings also sustained damage during the unrest. The Maryland Transit Administration (MTA) reported damage to buses and light rail vehicles.

Community Reaction. Following the violence, Black residents expressed fear, uncertainty and anger over the circumstances surrounding Freddie Gray's death and the response from law enforcement. Some stated that they felt their neighborhood was no longer safe.

Tourism Affected. Also, the negative publicity and ongoing unrest during the immediate aftermath of Freddie Gray's death had a detrimental impact on Baltimore's image as a tourist destination and commercial hub. Events and conventions were canceled or postponed, impacting the local economy and businesses that rely on tourism and visitor spending.

<u>Police Reform.</u> The protests and subsequent unrest amplified calls for police reform and increased accountability within the Baltimore Police Department (BPD). Civil rights groups demanded transparency in investigations of police-involved incidents and for addressing systemic issues of racial bias and excessive use of force.

<u>Civil Rights Investigation.</u> The U.S. Department of Justice (DOJ) conducted an investigation into the BPD's practices, leading to a report that found systemic issues of unconstitutional policing, racial discrimination and excessive force. This investigation ultimately resulted in a consent decree between the DOJ and the City of Baltimore in 2017.

<u>Consent Decree.</u> The consent decree outlined a comprehensive set of reforms designed to address systemic issues identified in the DOJ investigation. These reforms spanned various aspects of policing, including use of force policies, training, community engagement, accountability measures and data collection.

In addition, the consent decree provided for an independent monitor, appointed by the court and approved by both the city and the DOJ, to oversee implementation of the consent decree.

The consent decree emphasized the importance of community engagement and transparency in the reform process. It required the BPD to establish mechanisms for soliciting feedback from community members and stakeholders on policing practices and departmental policies.

The decree placed significant emphasis on enhancing training programs for officers, particularly in areas related to de-escalation techniques, bias-free policing and interactions with vulnerable populations.

The consent decree also included accountability measures to ensure that officers who engage in misconduct are held responsible through fair and transparent disciplinary processes. The BPD was required to develop and implement new policies and procedures that align with constitutional standards and best practices in law enforcement. These policies cover a wide range of areas, including use of force, stops, searches and arrests.

No Federal Crime. In September 2017, the DOJ announced that it would not pursue federal civil rights charges, concluding that there was insufficient evidence to support the level of proof required to sustain federal charges against the officers.

State Criminal Charges. Six officers (5 male and 1 female) involved in Freddie Gray's arrest and transport faced state charges alleging various offenses including assault, manslaughter, misconduct in office and second-degree depraved heart murder.

The trials of the officers took place over the course of 2015 and 2016 with all officers either being acquitted or having their charges dropped.

Renewed Debate. The trials and their outcomes sparked heated public debate and demonstrations in Baltimore and across the United States, highlighting issues of police accountability, racial justice and the use of force by law enforcement.

The fallout from the court proceedings included citizen demonstrations across the country where protesters peacefully expressed disappointment and frustration with the trial outcomes, advocating for justice and reforms in policing.

Further Protests. Some protests escalated into incidents of civil unrest, including isolated incidents of violence, vandalism and clashes with law enforcement, but not on the scale of the original violence.

Long-term Effects

Renewed Activism. The Baltimore protests sparked renewed activism and calls for systemic change within the city. Community organizations and activists continued to push for police accountability, racial justice and investment in underserved neighborhoods.

National Audience. The protests in Baltimore also garnered national attention and became a focal point in the broader movement for police reform and racial justice reigniting debates about systemic racism and inequality in American society.

Baltimore Today

Income Disparities. The median incomes in Baltimore today still reflect large racial disparities with the median household income for White households being $85,027 while the Black household median income stands at only $45,420.

Policing Disparities. There continue to be concerns about racial disparities in policing practices, including stop-and-frisk policies, use of force incidents and allegations of racial profiling. Efforts to improve police accountability and transparency, such as the implementation of body-worn cameras and the community oversight mechanisms mandated by the 2017 Consent Decree, continue amid unflagging calls for systemic reforms.

Justice Imbalances. Baltimore's Black residents are still disproportionately represented in the criminal justice system, from arrests to sentencing and incarceration rates. And the impact of policies like mandatory minimum sentencing and disparities in access to legal representation contributes to systemic inequities.

Employment Inequality. Segregation and historical disinvestment in predominantly Black neighborhoods contribute to continuing disparities in employment opportunities and wage levels. Limited access to quality education and job training programs exacerbates economic inequality within communities of color.

Segregation. Redlining and discriminatory housing practices in the past continue to affect residential segregation and access to affordable housing options. Gentrification and housing market dynamics often displace long-term residents, disproportionately impacting Black communities. In fact, residential segregation is so well defined that, in Baltimore today, racism has a shape.

Black Butterfly. Through the middle of the city, a land tract in the shape of an L contains the White neighborhoods where amenities and advantages—from bikeshare stations to bank branches—cluster. On either side of the White L, the Black neighborhoods extend in the shape of a butterfly. There, the manifestation of decades of intentional and structural disadvantage are evident: lower quality grocery stores, highways built through neighborhoods, and behind the homes and schools, a history of redlining and chronic disinvestment. [Tableau, Omar Ablassi August 6, 2021]

Healthcare. Black residents in Baltimore continue to face disparities in access to healthcare services, leading to higher rates of chronic illnesses like diabetes and lower life expectancy compared to other racial groups.

Political Injustice. Ongoing efforts to suppress voter participation and gerrymandering practices disproportionately impact Black voters in Baltimore. Challenges in achieving equitable political representation and influence remain significant concerns.

Renewed Activism. On a more positive note, grassroots organizations and advocacy groups in Baltimore continue to mobilize efforts to address systemic racism through policy advocacy, community empowerment and direct-action campaigns. Other initiatives focus on promoting racial equity, social justice and inclusive economic development to address long-standing disparities. Some examples of these organizations and initiatives are as follows:

The Black Butterfly Academy. Led by Dr. Lawrence Brown, this initiative focuses on addressing racial equity and the impacts of historical trauma on community health. It offers training, consulting and community engagement to foster understanding and action against systemic racism [Tableau].

Baltimore Racial Justice Action (BRJA). BRJA is dedicated to dismantling racism and promoting racial justice through education, advocacy and community organizing. They offer workshops, training sessions and resources to help individuals and organizations address and combat racism [Tableau].

The Center for Urban Health Equity at Morgan State University. This new center, where Dr. Lawrence Brown is an incoming Community Research Scholar, aims to improve the health and well-being of urban populations through research, community engagement and policy advocacy. It focuses on addressing health disparities that disproportionately affect Black residents [Tableau].

Baltimore Neighborhood Indicators Alliance (BNIA). BNIA provides data and analysis to support neighborhood-level improvements in quality of life. Their work includes highlighting disparities and informing policies to promote equity and justice across Baltimore's communities [Tableau].

Baltimore Ceasefire 365. This grassroots movement aims to reduce violence in the city through peace-building activities, community outreach and support for residents affected by violence. Their work often intersects with broader efforts to address systemic issues contributing to violence, including poverty and lack of opportunities in Black communities [Tableau].

No Boundaries Coalition. This resident-led advocacy group works to address systemic injustices in Central West Baltimore. Their initiatives include voter engagement, public safety advocacy and efforts to improve food access and health services for Black residents [Tableau].

Black Philanthropy Circle. This initiative, launched by the Baltimore Community Foundation, provides financial support to organizations that directly benefit Black residents. Recent grant recipients include ABC Park Seminoles Sports Agency, B360, Baltimore Hunger Project, and Fight Blight Bmore. The goal is not just financial support but also offering networking and other resources to help these organizations thrive.

Baltimore Children & Youth Fund (BCYF). The BCYF supports youth-centered organizations and initiatives. It aims to empower young people through grants, capacity-building programs and community engagement efforts. The BCYF collaborates with grassroots organizations and community leaders to ensure that children and youth have access to a range of enriching programs.

CLLCTIVLY. CLLCTIVLY builds an ecosystem of grants and resources to support Black-led organizations in Baltimore. It offers a directory of Black-led social enterprises and acts as a hub for resources aimed at improving the city.

Black Yield Institute. Focused on food justice, this grassroots organization works to provide healthful food options in underserved neighborhoods. It collaborates with local farmers and community members to create sustainable food systems and address food insecurity.

B-360. This nonprofit uses the city's dirt bike culture to teach engineering skills to youth. It also serves as a diversion program for young people involved in illegal dirt bike riding, aiming to transform their interests into productive activities.

Fight Blight Bmore. This organization tackles the issue of vacant properties in Baltimore by identifying and advocating for the renovation or demolition of these spaces. Their data-driven approach helps highlight the effects of disinvestment and marginalization in Black communities.

Pass IT On. Pas IT ON is a nonprofit organization aiming to diversify the IT field and close the technology skills gap impacting disadvantaged communities. It provides STEM and workforce development training to help bridge the divide in the tech sector.

Project Own. Focused on increasing homeownership among Black residents, Project Own offers financial readiness programs in partnership with Neighborhood Housing Services of Baltimore. It addresses the disparity in homeownership rates and aims to improve socioeconomic mobility and wealth creation.

Conclusion

The Baltimore protests of 2015, catalyzed by the tragic death of Freddie Gray while in police custody, brought to the forefront longstanding grievances rooted in systemic racism, socioeconomic disparities and police-community relations. These demonstrations, known as the Baltimore Uprising, underscored deep-seated issues that have historically marginalized Black communities in the city.

Historical injustices such as racial zoning laws, redlining and urban renewal projects have perpetuated segregation, economic inequality and disenfranchisement among Black residents in Baltimore. These systemic barriers have contributed to disparities in education, healthcare, employment and housing opportunities, exacerbating social inequities across generations.

Freddie Gray's death served as a triggering incident that ignited a wave of protests demanding justice and police accountability. While many demonstrations (perhaps even most) were peaceful, tensions escalated into instances of violence, looting and property damage, prompting a state of emergency declaration and deployment of National Guard troops.

The aftermath of the protests prompted a national dialogue on police reform and racial justice, leading to a Department of Justice investigation and a subsequent consent decree mandating reforms within the Baltimore Police Department. These efforts aim to address issues of excessive force, racial profiling and community engagement, although challenges persist in achieving lasting systemic change.

Today, Baltimore continues to grapple with the legacies of systemic racism reflected in disparities in income, education, healthcare and criminal justice outcomes. Despite ongoing challenges, grassroots movements and advocacy groups remain steadfast in their efforts to advocate for equity, transparency and inclusive policies that uplift and empower marginalized communities.

The legacy of the Baltimore protests serves as a reminder of the ongoing struggle for racial justice and equality in American cities, underscoring the imperative for sustained efforts to dismantle systemic racism and create inclusive opportunities for all residents.

CHAPTER FOURTEEN

THE GEORGE FLOYD PROTESTS OF 2020

The George Floyd Protests of 2020 were a series of widespread demonstrations and civil unrest that swept across the United States and around the world in response to the killing of George Floyd, a Black man, by Minneapolis police officer Derek Chauvin on May 25, 2020. Following is a detailed overview of the causes, key incidents and aftermath of the protests.

Background

Although Minneapolis certainly featured multiple examples of all forms of racism in 2020, the particular complaint at the forefront in the George Floyd protests was police brutality. Several specific occurrences had garnered considerable public attention to this issue.

Jamar Clark. On November 15, 2015, Jamar Clark, a 24-year-old Black man, was involved in a domestic disturbance call in North Minneapolis. Police responded to a report of a woman being assaulted by a man who was interfering with paramedics attempting to provide medical aid.

Officers Mark Ringgenberg and Dustin Schwarze arrived at the scene and encountered Jamar Clark. According to police accounts, Clark was interfering with emergency responders and became confrontational. Officers attempted to restrain Clark, leading to a struggle.

During the altercation, both officers claimed that Clark had gained control of one of their firearms and that they feared for their lives. Schwarze shot Clark once in the head. Clark was taken to the Hennepin County Medical Center and was pronounced dead the next day.

According to some witnesses and community members, Clark was handcuffed at the time of the shooting. They claimed that he was already restrained and posed no immediate threat to the officers when lethal force was used against him. However, the officers involved in the incident insisted that Clark was not handcuffed during the altercation and some witnesses supported the officers' version of events.

The exact circumstances surrounding whether Jamar Clark was handcuffed remain a point of contention and were a significant factor in the public outcry and protests that followed the incident. The Minnesota Bureau of Criminal Apprehension conducted an investigation into the shooting, and the Hennepin County Attorney ultimately decided not to pursue criminal charges against the officers involved, citing a lack of evidence to prove the charges "beyond a reasonable doubt" and noting that some witness statements supported the officers' account of the events.

This substantial dispute as to the facts fueled immediate outrage and allegations of excessive force and police misconduct.

Philando Castile. Although not part of Minneapolis itself, the nearby suburb of Falcon Heights saw the shooting of Philando Castile on July 6, 2016. Castile, a 32-year-old unarmed Black man, was pulled over for a broken taillight and shot by a police officer while reaching for his identification, as police had instructed.

The aftermath, including the live-streamed video of Castile bleeding in his car, sparked protests and renewed discussions about police use of force and racial bias.

Thurman Blevins. On June 23, 2018, officers responded to a report of a man firing a handgun into the air. On their arrival at the scene they found Thurman Blevins, a 31-year-old Black man, in possession of a handgun. Blevins ran.

Officers reported that, during the foot chase, Blevins was holding a handgun and did not comply with commands to drop it. They further stated that Blevins turned toward the officers and pointed the gun in their direction, prompting them to open fire. Police fired multiple rounds. Blevins was hit four times in the back and fell dead at the scene.

Witnesses and community members contested the police account, arguing that Blevins was running away from the officers and did not pose an immediate threat when he was shot. Body camera footage appeared to contradict the officers' accounts and simply showed Blevins trying to run away.

The shooting of Thurman Blevins sparked protests and renewed calls for police accountability and reform in Minneapolis.

Daunte Wright. Daunte Wright was a 20-year-old Black man who was fatally shot by police officer Kimberly Potter during a traffic stop in the Minneapolis suburb of Brooklyn Center, Minnesota, on April 11, 2021.

During the traffic stop, officers discovered that Wright had an outstanding warrant for a misdemeanor weapons charge. As the officers attempted to arrest him, Wright tried to get back into his car. Potter, a veteran officer with 26 years of experience, drew her service weapon and shot Wright. She claimed she intended to use her Taser and mistakenly drew her gun instead. Although Potter was convicted of manslaughter, a sympathetic judge sentenced her to only two years in prison, a term that shocked the conscience of many Black residents in the community. She was free after serving 16 months.

Trigger Incident

It is against this violent background that, on May 25, 2020, Minneapolis Police arrested George Floyd, a 46-year-old Black man, outside Cup Foods, a convenience store in the Powderhorn Park neighborhood of Minneapolis. The police had been called after a store employee suspected Floyd of tendering a counterfeit $20 bill.

On arrival at the scene, the officers found George Floyd in his vehicle parked on the street outside Cup, where he was seated with two passengers. Officers ordered Floyd to exit the vehicle. Floyd voluntarily complied.

Reports and videos indicate that George Floyd initially refused to get into the police car. According to accounts, Floyd expressed reluctance and appeared distressed. This led to the officers attempting to restrain him on the ground, which ultimately culminated in the tragic events that followed.

Once Floyd was handcuffed on the ground, Officer Derek Chauvin knelt on Floyd's neck for approximately 9 minutes and 29 seconds, despite Floyd repeatedly stating that he could not breathe. Bystander video footage showed Floyd pleading for his life and calling out for his mother. During the restraint, Floyd became unresponsive.

Despite bystanders' pleas to check Floyd's pulse and provide medical assistance, the officers maintained their positions until an ambulance arrived. Floyd was then taken to Hennepin County Medical Center, where he was pronounced dead on arrival.

The Protests

<u>Video Evidence Disseminated.</u> The first protests began in Minneapolis, where George Floyd was killed, with community members demanding justice for Floyd and accountability for the officers involved in his death. Videos of the arrest hit the internet and the protests quickly spread to other cities across the United States.

<u>Nationwide Expansion.</u> The protests expanded rapidly, with millions of people taking to the streets in cities and towns across all 50 states showing their outrage of Floyd's treatment at the hands of law enforcement. The protests were largely peaceful but occasionally turned violent, with clashes between protesters and law enforcement, as well as instances of looting and property damage.

<u>International Response.</u> The Minneapolis protests sparked solidarity demonstrations in cities around the world, including in countries such as the United Kingdom, Canada, Australia, France, Germany and South Africa. Protesters rallied behind the Black Lives Matter movement and called for an end to racial injustice and police violence.

<u>Escalation.</u> As tensions grew and demands for police accountability were not met swiftly, some protests escalated into riots and widespread civil unrest in Minneapolis. The unrest began around May 27, 2020, and continued for several days.

<u>Precinct Targeted.</u> Early in the unrest, rioters targeted and set fire to the Third Police Precinct building in Minneapolis, which was eventually evacuated and abandoned by officers. Instances of violence, including clashes between protesters and police, as well as looting of businesses, were reported throughout the city for several days.

<u>Outside Elements.</u> Outsiders seemed to rally quickly to the unrest, coming from many places to join the protests and chaos. Incoming protestors brought with them "outside agitators" who participated in

the looting and violent clashes with police. One television news report showed video of a group of five White men and women breaking windows and looting a pharmacy. No Black looters were visible on the video.

National Guard Deployed. On May 28th, Minnesota Governor Tim Walz ordered the deployment of about 500 National Guard Troops to help quell the violence and restore order. Over the next several days that number increased dramatically to about 7,000. This deployment was one of the largest in Minnesota's history and reflected the severity of the situation.

At the same time, Governor Walz also asked U.S. President Donald J. Trump to send support from federal law enforcement agencies. President Trump responded by deploying approximately 100 personnel from the FBI, ATF and U.S. Marshals Service.

Police Tactics. Minneapolis Police used tear gas, shield lines, rubber bullets and water cannons in attempts to control and disperse the rioting crowds. Guard troops lent support to MPD by patrolling streets and helping to enforce curfews.

At least as important as the actions taken by police were actions the police chose to forego. The most notable example was at the Third Precinct where police chose to vacate the building rather than stand and fight with the rioters. There were several other significant instances where police officers pulled back from confrontations with protesters to de-escalate situations. These tactical retreats were aimed at preventing violent clashes and reducing the potential for injuries.

The police decision to give ground was met with mixed reactions. Some community leaders and residents supported the approach as a way to prevent further violence and destruction. Others criticized it, arguing that it allowed for unchecked vandalism and looting, which further destabilized the city.

Gradual End. Over the following weeks, a combination of law enforcement efforts, community engagement, legal measures and societal responses contributed to the gradual cessation of the unrest. Extensive media coverage and public awareness of the protests and their underlying issues also helped bring calm to the Minneapolis streets.

Immediate Impact

Casualties. Two men died during the Minneapolis riots. One was fatally shot by a shop owner who has claimed self-defense. The other died in the arson of his pawn shop during the riot.

Property Damage. The property damage during the George Floyd protests in Minneapolis was extensive. Estimates indicate that the damage exceeded $500 million, making it the second-most destructive incident of civil unrest in U.S. history, after the 1992 Los Angeles riots. More than 1,500 buildings in Minneapolis and St. Paul were damaged or destroyed. This included businesses, homes and public buildings, with many structures being completely burned down.

Extent of Destruction. The destruction ranged from minor vandalism and broken windows to complete destruction by fire. Several businesses were looted and set ablaze, leading to significant economic impact on the affected communities.

Economic Impact. The economic impact of the property damage was substantial. Many small business owners faced severe financial losses, and the cost of rebuilding and repairs added to the overall economic burden on the Twin Cities.

Insurance Claims. Standard property/casualty insurance policies at the time of the Floyd Protests covered damage caused by rioting and civil unrest, unlike those in force at the time of the Tulsa Massacre. And insurance claims related to the damage were significant, with insurance companies facing payouts in the hundreds of millions of dollars to cover the losses incurred by property owners.

Murder Trial. In the months following Floyd's murder, Derek Chauvin, the police officer who knelt on George Floyd's neck, was charged with second-degree unintentional murder, third-degree murder and second-degree manslaughter. On April 20, 2021, a Minneapolis jury consisting of White people, Black people and multi-racial citizens found Chauvin guilty on all charges. The verdict was met with relief and celebration by many protesters.

On June 25, 2021, Hennepin County District Court Judge Peter Cahill handed down Chauvin's state sentences, as follows.

--22.5 years for second-degree unintentional murder;

--15 years for third-degree murder; and

--10 years for second-degree Manslaughter.

He is serving his sentences concurrently.

Civil Rights Sentence. On July 7, 2022, a federal judge also sentenced Chauvin to 22.5 years in federal prison for violating Floyd's civil rights. This sentence is being served concurrently with Chauvin's state prison terms.

Long-term Effects

The George Floyd protests reignited calls for sweeping reforms to address systemic issues of police brutality and racial bias within law enforcement. Demands included reallocating funding from police departments to social services, implementing community policing practices, "defunding" the police and holding officers accountable for misconduct.

Historical Significance. The George Floyd protests of 2020 are widely viewed as one of the largest and most significant social movements in modern American history. The protests brought renewed attention to issues of racial injustice and police violence, sparking a national reckoning on systemic racism and inequality.

Cultural/Artistic Expressions. The protests also inspired a wave of cultural and artistic expressions, including murals, songs, films and literature, highlighting the Black Lives Matter movement and the fight for racial justice. The phrase "I can't breathe," which became a rallying cry for protesters, symbolized the struggle against police brutality and racial oppression.

Political Effects. Further, the protests had significant political ramifications, influencing the 2020 presidential election and shaping public discourse on issues of racial justice and social equity. The movement also spurred legislative action at the local, state and federal levels, with lawmakers introducing bills aimed at addressing systemic racism and police reform.

Minneapolis Today

In 2024, systemic racism against Black individuals in Minneapolis remains a significant issue, impacting various facets of life such as education, employment, health and housing.

Major racial disparities in median income continue to be a concern in 2024, with median White households receiving $87,057 and median Black households only receiving $37,494.

Education. Racial disparities in education are particularly stark. Black students in Minnesota, including Minneapolis, face significant opportunity gaps from early childhood through postsecondary education. These gaps manifest in lower readiness for kindergarten, higher disciplinary rates, lower test scores and reduced college attainment compared to their White peers. This educational inequity ultimately contributes to broader income disparities later in life.

Health and Housing. Health disparities also persist, with Black Minnesotans facing higher rates of chronic diseases and reduced access to quality healthcare. In housing, discriminatory practices and historical redlining have contributed to significant gaps in homeownership rates and living conditions between Black and White residents. Organizations and community leaders are actively working to address these issues through various programs and legislative efforts.

Employment and Income. Black residents in Minneapolis continue to experience higher unemployment rates and lower wage incomes compared to White residents. Efforts to address these disparities include initiatives aimed at fostering economic growth and job creation within the Black community. Some examples include:

Northside Economic Opportunity Network (NEON). NEON supports entrepreneurs of color by providing business development services, including training, technical assistance and access to financing. The organization aims to reduce economic disparities by helping Black business owners and entrepreneurs succeed.

Metropolitan Economic Development Association (MEDA). MEDA offers consulting services, access to capital, and business development support for minority-owned businesses. Their programs include financial education, loan programs and access to business resources to help Black entrepreneurs grow and sustain their businesses.

The Minneapolis Foundation's Strategic Framework. This foundation focuses on equity and inclusion, providing grants and support for initiatives that aim to reduce racial disparities in education, housing and economic opportunities. They have funded various programs that support job training, employment services and business development for the Black community.

Twin Cities R!SE. Twin Cities R!SE provides comprehensive job training and placement services, particularly focusing on underrepresented communities. Their programs help Black residents gain skills and secure employment, addressing barriers such as transportation, childcare and housing that can impede job success.

The Black Women's Wealth Alliance (BWWA). The Black Women's Wealth Alliance was founded in 2014 by Kenya McKnight-Ahad. BWWA focuses on building wealth among Black women through financial literacy, business development and investment education. Their programs include workshops, mentoring and access to capital, helping Black women entrepreneurs build and grow their businesses.

Hennepin County Workforce Development. Hennepin County offers various workforce development programs aimed at increasing employment opportunities for Black residents. These programs include job fairs, training workshops and partnerships with local businesses to provide job placements and internships.

Target Corporation's Initiatives. Target has committed to increasing its investments in Black-owned businesses and suppliers. The company also aims to increase representation in its workforce and provide career development opportunities for Black employees.

All Square. All Square is a nonprofit social enterprise in Minneapolis that focuses on supporting individuals impacted by mass incarceration. The organization combines a unique blend of a grilled cheese restaurant, legal support and professional development programs to help formerly incarcerated people reintegrate into society and achieve personal and professional growth.

The grilled cheese restaurant serves as both a community hub and an economic engine. It provides competitive jobs in a welcoming environment for people re-entering society after incarceration. The profits from the restaurant support All Square's Fellowship and Prison to Law Pipeline programs.

All Square's fellowship program is designed exclusively for individuals impacted by the criminal justice system. It focuses on employment, wellness, and creative skills development. Fellows receive support through therapy sessions, legal services and professional development opportunities.

Prison-to-Law Pipeline. All Square aims to empower incarcerated and formerly incarcerated individuals by providing access to paralegal and juris doctorate degrees. This initiative is part of the broader Legal Revolution effort, which seeks to transform the legal system by involving those most affected by it.

Overall, All Square exemplifies a holistic approach to criminal justice reform, combining social enterprise with educational and legal support to create meaningful opportunities for those affected by mass incarceration.

City of Minneapolis' Inclusive Economic Development Policy. The city's policy focuses on creating equitable economic opportunities by supporting minority-owned businesses, investing in affordable housing and ensuring equitable access to city contracts and resources. This policy is designed to address systemic barriers and promote economic inclusion.

Community and Legislative Efforts. In response to these ongoing challenges, over 80 organizations in Minnesota's Black community have launched the Alliance of Alliances, a collaborative initiative aimed at addressing these systemic disparities. The details regarding this organization bear detailed recognition.

The Alliance of Alliances. The Alliance of Alliances in Minneapolis is an expansive coalition of organizations working together to address systemic issues and promote equity and justice within the city. This coalition brings together diverse groups with the aim of leveraging their collective strengths to create a more significant impact on community challenges, particularly those related to racial and economic disparities.

Collaborative Advocacy. The Alliance of Alliances aims to amplify the voices of marginalized communities by fostering collaboration among various advocacy groups. This helps to present a united front when addressing issues of systemic racism, economic inequality and social injustice.

Resource Sharing. By pooling resources, member organizations can provide more comprehensive support to the communities they serve. This includes sharing financial resources, expertise and networks to enhance the effectiveness of their initiatives.

Policy Influence. The coalition works to influence local and state policies by engaging in collective lobbying efforts. This involves pushing for legislative changes that address the root causes of law enforcement disparities affecting Black residents and other marginalized groups in Minneapolis.

Community Empowerment. Empowering local communities through education, training and capacity-building programs is a key focus. These efforts help individuals gain the skills and knowledge needed to advocate for themselves and their communities.

Joint Campaigns. The Alliance of Alliances organizes joint campaigns on issues such as affordable housing, criminal justice reform and economic development. These campaigns are designed to raise awareness, mobilize community members and push for systemic change.

Public Forums and Workshops. The Alliance holds regular public forums and workshops to engage the community, discuss pressing issues and develop strategic plans for collective action. These events provide platforms for sharing information, experiences and strategies.

Research and Reports. The coalition conducts research and publishes reports on the state of systemic racism and other related issues in Minneapolis. These reports are used to inform policy recommendations and advocacy efforts.

Support Services. Providing direct support services such as legal assistance, job training and business development programs to community members is another critical component of their work.

Member Organizations. The Alliance of Alliances consists of various local organizations, each with its unique focus and expertise. While specific member organizations can vary, they generally include:

Civil rights organizations;

Community development groups;

Economic empowerment entities;

Health and wellness advocates; and

Educational institutions.

The Alliance focuses on creating solutions developed by and for the Black community, emphasizing the need for support from both the private sector and public officials.

Conclusion

The George Floyd protests of 2020 marked a pivotal moment in the fight against systemic racism and police brutality in the United States and around the world. Triggered by the tragic death of George Floyd at the hands of a Minneapolis police officer, these protests brought to the forefront the longstanding issues of racial injustice and the urgent need for comprehensive police reform.

The outrage was not only a response to the killing of George Floyd but also a cumulative reaction to a series of similar incidents, including the deaths of Jamar Clark, Philando Castile, Daunte Wright and Thurman Blevins. Each of these cases highlighted the persistent issues of excessive force and racial bias within law enforcement, igniting demands for accountability and change.

The immediate impacts of the protests were significant. Derek Chauvin's conviction and sentencing represented a rare instance of accountability for police violence, offering a measure of justice for George Floyd's death. The widespread demonstrations also spurred legislative and policy initiatives aimed at addressing police misconduct and broader racial disparities. At the federal, state and local levels, lawmakers introduced bills to reform policing practices, improve accountability and address systemic racism.

Despite these efforts, systemic racism in Minneapolis remains a critical issue in 2024, manifesting in significant disparities across various sectors such as education, health, housing and employment. Black residents continue to face higher unemployment rates, lower incomes and poorer health outcomes compared to their White counterparts. The education system still shows significant opportunity gaps, and discriminatory practices in housing persist.

However, numerous initiatives are actively working to bridge these gaps and foster economic growth within the Black community. Organizations like NEON, MEDA and the Black Women's Wealth Alliance provide crucial support to Black entrepreneurs, while programs like Twin Cities R!SE and Hennepin County Workforce Development aim to improve employment opportunities. The Minneapolis

Foundation and Target Corporation have also committed resources to addressing racial disparities.

The Alliance of Alliances stands out as a significant collaborative effort, bringing together over 80 organizations to tackle systemic issues collectively. By focusing on collaborative advocacy, resource sharing, policy influence and community empowerment, this coalition represents a concerted effort to create lasting change in Minneapolis.

In conclusion, while the George Floyd protests catalyzed essential conversations and actions around racial justice, the journey towards true equity in Minneapolis is ongoing. The collective efforts of community organizations, policymakers and activists continue to be crucial in dismantling systemic racism and building a more just and inclusive society.

CHAPTER FIFTEEN

CONCLUSION

This book has presented a brief history of incidents of civil unrest in America. We've explored the circumstances that underly the various disturbances, the triggering incidents and the short and long-term effect of the unrest. We've also seen contemporary snapshots of the cities where each incident of unrest occurred and highlighted remaining challenges to combat systemic racism as well as initiatives and efforts to address those challenges.

We have revealed characteristics unique to each event of unrest, as well as circumstances shared by many:

New York City Draft Riots (1863). Unhappy with the favoritism shown to the wealthy in the civil war draft, predominantly White mobs targeted Black residents, resulting in at least 119 deaths.

Marking an early use of federal army troops to control domestic unrest, this riot contributed to the future trend of an increasingly militarized police force. Underlying causes of the racial tensions included labor market competition, racial animosity and prejudice. Inflammatory newspaper headlines set the stage for the violence, along with resentment of the idea of Black people gaining freedom and equality or holding equal social status.

Atlanta Race Riot (1906). Fueled by sensationalized newspaper reports of alleged assaults by Black men on White women, a White mob attacked Black Atlanta killing dozens and injuring many more.

This riot illustrated how sensationalized anti-Black propaganda can trigger White mob violence against Black people. Common themes of systemic racism—discrimination in jobs, wages, education and healthcare—coupled with perceived discrimination by the police, would repeat themselves again and again in future incidents of unrest.

One result of this riot was the formation of the NAACP in 1909.

East St. Louis Riot (1917). Tensions between local White workers and Black workers (who had migrated to the North during the Great Migration) erupted in East St. Louis, Illinois. With the violence leaving an estimated 39 to 150 Black residents dead and causing extensive property damage, this was one of the most lethal riots in American history.

Incited by a solitary act of retribution by a Black resident and blown out of proportion by rumors that spread like wildfire, the rioting saw White people vandalizing and burning Black-owned properties and lynching Black residents.

The East St. Louis Riot marked an early use of the National Guard to assist local authorities in restoring calm in a case of unrest, although federal army troops also participated.

Chicago Race Riot (1919). Part of the "Red Summer" of 1919, the Chicago riot began when a Black teenager drowned after being stoned by White beachgoers. The violence, which lasted for days, resulted in 38 deaths and over 500 injuries.

The riot began on the South Side of Chicago and quickly spread, with White mobs attacking Black neighborhoods and Black individuals defending themselves and their communities. By the end, thousands of Black people were left homeless and extensive property damage had occurred, particularly in Black neighborhoods but also as a result of retaliatory attacks in White communities.

The Chicago Race Riot of 1919 was a pivotal moment in the early civil rights movement. The NAACP and other organizations used the riot to push for federal anti-lynching legislation and greater civil rights protections. No anti-lynching laws were ever enacted at the federal level.

Tulsa Race Massacre (1921). One of the most devastating race riots in U.S. history occurred in Tulsa, Oklahoma, where a White mob attacked the prosperous Black neighborhood of Greenwood, known as "Black Wall Street." The violence killed an estimated 100 to 300 Black residents, destroyed hundreds of homes and businesses, and completely decimated the community.

Spawned by racist rumors and incendiary media reports, White rioters destroyed an estimated 35 city blocks in Greenwood. For the first time on record, private planes were employed to drop incendiary devices from the air to enhance the effects of a riot.

Only recently, has the massacre emerged from the shadows of "omissionist" American history, receiving its due attention as the subject of corrected history books, storybooks, documentaries and other forms of media, and bringing greater awareness to this dark chapter in American history.

Detroit Race Riot (1943). Longstanding racial tensions in Detroit, Michigan erupted into violence in June 1943. False rumors of Black men attacking White women triggered the attacks against Black residents and their property. Between 34 and 43 people died (mostly Black) with more than 1,800 sustaining injuries. Police also reported more than 1,800 arrests.

Underpinned by employment competition between Black people moving north during The Great Migration and White people returning from WWII, the riot became a rallying point for civil rights activists who sought to address racial discrimination and police brutality.

Watts Riots (1965). Sparked by an incident of police brutality in the Watts neighborhood of Los Angeles, California, the riots lasted six days, resulting in 34 deaths and over a thousand injuries. Hundreds of buildings were damaged or destroyed, including homes, businesses and public facilities.

The Watts Riots mark an early incident where Black people, not White people, were major instigators of the unrest. The riots particularly highlighted incidents of police brutality and the need for law enforcement reform.

In its review of the Watts Riots, the Kerner Commission's report concluded that the nation was "moving toward two societies, one Black, one White—separate and unequal," identifying systemic racism, economic inequality and inadequate housing, education and employment opportunities as root causes of urban unrest. The report called for comprehensive federal initiatives to address racial disparities, improve urban infrastructure and enhance social services. It also emphasized the need for better community relations and policing reforms.

Newark and Detroit Riots (1967). Part of what became known as "The Long, Hot Summer," widespread racial unrest boiled over in Newark, New Jersey and Detroit, Michigan. Police brutality and deep-seated racial inequalities lay at the heart of both uprisings. The Newark riots resulted in 26 deaths, while the Detroit riots left 43 dead.

The riots caused extensive property damage, estimated at over $40 million (equivalent to around $330 million today). Thousands of buildings were destroyed or severely damaged, leaving large swaths of Black Detroit a desolate wasteland. The riot also accelerated "White flight" from urban areas, contributing to the overall economic decline of Detroit.

The riots marked the first recorded occurrence of military tanks for crowd control. It is important to note that many of the rights rioters demanded were already guaranteed to them by federal legislation, such as the Civil Rights Act of 1964.

Miami Riot (1980). The acquittal of four White police officers who had beaten a Black motorcyclist to death sparked riots in Miami, Florida. The violence resulted in 18 deaths, over 350 injuries and approximately 600 arrests.

The riot caused extensive property damage, estimated at around $380 million in today's dollars. Hundreds of businesses were looted and burned, leaving many blocks of Liberty City and Overtown in ruins.

The beating death of Arthur McDuffie at the hands of police became a symbol of police brutality and the racial injustices faced by Black people in America leading to ever more ardent calls for police reform and greater accountability for law enforcement officers.

Outside Elements. Of the riots covered in this book, the Miami Riot was the first to feature substantial outside elements such as agitators, opportunistic criminals and those seeking to exploit the unrest for reasons known only to themselves.

Los Angeles Riots (1992). Following the acquittal of four LAPD officers filmed beating Rodney King, widespread riots broke out in Los Angeles, California. The riots resulted in 63 deaths, over 2,000 injuries and more than $1 billion in property damage—the greatest dollar damage caused by any rioting to date.

The riots marked an early use of federal law enforcement officers, instead of army troops, to assist local authorities in controlling violence and restoring calm.

The stark video account of the Rodney King incident caused a nationwide crisis of trust between Black citizens and the police who patrolled their neighborhoods, prompting renewed calls for law enforcement reform.

The federal Civil Rights trial of the LA Police officers marked a new avenue of federal intervention in a case of alleged police brutality.

<u>Ferguson Unrest (2014).</u> The shooting death of Michael Brown, an unarmed Black teenager, by a White police officer in Ferguson, Missouri, led to protests and riots, highlighting issues of police brutality and racial discrimination.

In the post-Rodney King world, national tolerance for police brutality waned, leading to widely-broadcast attention to the peaceful protests in Ferguson that may have gone unreported a few decades earlier.

A major dispute about the prosecutor's use of the grand jury system led to outcries for justice reform.

Additionally, the Ferguson Unrest featured an early use of a consent decree between the city and the U.S. Department of Justice to mandate reforms in the police department and municipal court system, including providing for ongoing federal monitoring and enforcement.

<u>Baltimore Protests (2015).</u> The death of Freddie Gray, a Black man who died from injuries sustained while in police custody, sparked protests and riots in Baltimore, Maryland.

The protests and subsequent unrest amplified calls for police reform and increased accountability within the Baltimore Police Department. But criminal proceedings prosecuted against five accused officers rendered zero convictions.

<u>George Floyd Protests (2020).</u> The murder of George Floyd, an unarmed Black man, by a Minneapolis police officer ignited nationwide protests and riots against police brutality and systemic racism, becoming one of the largest protest movements in U.S. history.

A verdict of "guilty on all charges" and the subsequent sentencing of police officer, Derek Chauvin, to 22.5 years in prison marked a rare conviction of an officer in a murder case involving police brutality.

Although not the first instance of using federal Civil Rights charges to imprison police officers, Chauvin's Civil Rights conviction and 22.5-year sentence for violating George Floyd's civil rights provided confirmation that the federal justice system was taking police violence seriously—a welcome change from decades past.

Overarching Themes and Patterns in U.S. Race Riots

Racial Tensions and Economic Competition. One recurring theme across these riots is the significant racial tension fueled by economic competition. In many cases, such as the New York City Draft Riots (1863) and the East St. Louis Riot (1917), the arrival of Black workers in Northern cities during the Great Migration sparked conflicts over jobs and housing. White workers often perceived Black newcomers as economic threats and lesser humans leading to violent confrontations.

Sensationalized Media and Rumors. Sensationalized media reports and inflammatory rumors played crucial roles in inciting violence. The Atlanta Race Riot (1906) was triggered by false allegations of Black men assaulting White women, and similarly, the Tulsa Race Massacre (1921) was fueled by racist rumors and incendiary media reports. These instances highlight the destructive power of misinformation in escalating racial tensions.

Police Brutality and Lack of Accountability. Police brutality and the lack of accountability for law enforcement officers have been central to several riots, particularly in more recent events. The Watts Riots (1965), the Miami Riot (1980) and the George Floyd Protests (2020) were directly sparked by incidents of police violence against Black individuals. These events underscore the critical need for police reform and the pervasive distrust between Black communities and law enforcement.

Government Response and Military Involvement. The involvement of the military and federal government in quelling riots is another common pattern. The New York City Draft Riots (1863) marked an early use of federal troops for domestic unrest, a trend that continued with the National Guard's deployment during the East St. Louis Riot (1917), the Los Angeles Riots (1992) and most future occurrences of substantial civil unrest. This pattern illustrates the government's reliance on militarized responses to control civil disturbances, but also highlights the greater trust citizens have in the National Guard versus the local police to respect their civil rights.

Impact of Riots on Civil Rights Movement. Many of these riots had profound impacts on the civil rights movement and subsequent reforms. The Chicago Race Riot (1919) and the Detroit Race Riot (1943) became rallying points for civil rights activists advocating for federal anti-lynching legislation and greater protections for Black Americans. Although immediate legislative outcomes were often limited, these events raised national awareness and galvanized the fight for racial equality.

Persistent Socioeconomic Inequalities. Systemic racism, characterized by longstanding disparities in employment, housing, education and healthcare, underpins many of these riots. The Kerner Commission's report following the Watts Riots (1965) highlighted the deep-seated economic and social inequalities driving urban unrest. These disparities continue to manifest in various forms, as seen in the Baltimore Protests (2015) and the George Floyd Protests (2020), where calls for justice and equality remain urgent.

Evolving Nature of Riots. The nature of riots has evolved over time, reflecting broader societal changes. Early riots, such as the New York City Draft Riots and the Atlanta Race Riot, were predominantly instigated by White mobs targeting Black communities. In contrast, more recent events like the Watts Riots and the George Floyd Protests have seen Black communities taking the lead in expressing their frustrations through protests and, at times, violent unrest. This shift highlights the growing assertiveness of Black communities in demanding justice and accountability.

Conclusion

The purpose of this book was to provide a comprehensive analysis of civil unrest incidents in America, examining the causes, trigger, and impacts of these events, as well as contemporary snapshots of the cities affected and the ongoing challenges in combating systemic racism. Through this exploration, we have delved into the unique and shared characteristics of each event, revealing the complex interplay of racial tensions, economic competition, sensationalized media, police brutality and systemic inequalities that have fueled these riots over the years.

In reviewing the New York City Draft Riots (1863), the Atlanta Race Riot (1906), the East St. Louis Riot (1917), the Chicago Race Riot (1919), the Tulsa Race Massacre (1921), the Detroit Race Riot (1943), the Watts Riots (1965), the Newark and Detroit Riots (1967), the Miami Riot (1980), the Los Angeles Riots (1992), the Ferguson Unrest (2014), the Baltimore Protests (2015) and the George Floyd Protests (2020), we have uncovered several overarching themes and patterns. The significant racial tension driven by economic competition, the role of sensationalized media in inciting violence, the pervasive issue of police brutality and lack of accountability, the government's reliance on militarized responses, the profound impact on civil rights movements, and the persistent socioeconomic inequalities are recurring elements in these events.

The analysis highlights that while the nature of riots has evolved—from early events predominantly instigated by White mobs targeting Black communities to more recent protests led by Black communities demanding justice—the underlying issues remain deeply rooted. The evolution of these riots reflects broader societal changes and the growing assertiveness of Black communities in advocating for their rights and justice.

Addressing the root causes of these riots requires a multifaceted approach, including comprehensive economic and social reforms, improved media responsibility and significant changes in law enforcement practices. It is only through a sustained commitment to these areas that the cycle of racial unrest can be broken, paving the way for a more equitable and just society.

Finally, and most importantly, let the things you have learned from this book be a call to action. There is an urgent need for continued efforts to combat systemic racism. Each of us can do our part. Here are some ways:

Educate Yourself. You've already begun your education by reading this book. Continue to engage with literature on racism by reading books such as "White Fragility" by Robin DiAngelo, "How to Be an Antiracist" by Ibram X. Kendi and "The New Jim Crow" by Michelle Alexander.

Listen to Podcasts and Watch Documentaries. Resources like the "1619 Project" podcast or documentaries like "13th" by Ava DuVernay provide in-depth insights into the history and impact of systemic racism.

Examine Personal Biases. Reflect on and identify your own biases and prejudices. Tools like the Implicit Association Test (IAT) can help uncover unconscious biases.

<u>Acknowledge Privilege.</u> Recognize and understand the advantages you may have due to your race and how these advantages contribute to systemic inequality.

<u>Shop at Black-Owned Businesses.</u> Make a conscious effort to support Black entrepreneurs and businesses. Find them and buy from them.

<u>Donate to Organizations.</u> Contribute to organizations that work towards racial justice, such as the NAACP Legal Defense Fund, Black Lives Matter and local grassroots organizations like All Square in Minneapolis.

<u>Amplify Black Voices.</u> Use your platforms to share content created by Black individuals and amplify their voices on social media and in your community.

<u>Listen and Learn.</u> Prioritize listening to the experiences and perspectives of Black people without interjecting your own experiences or opinions.

<u>Advocate for Policy Changes.</u> Advocate for policies that address systemic racism, such as criminal justice reform, voting rights protection, and equitable education funding.

<u>Engage Politically.</u> Contact your representatives, participate in local government meetings, and vote for candidates who prioritize racial justice.

<u>Peaceful Protests.</u> Join peaceful protests and demonstrations to show solidarity and demand change.

<u>Community Organizing.</u> Get involved with local organizations that work towards racial equity and justice.

<u>Promote Diversity and Inclusion in the Workplace.</u> Advocate for fair hiring practices and support initiatives that promote diversity in the

workplace. Support or initiate anti-racism training and diversity workshops for employees.

Engage in Difficult Conversations. Challenge racist remarks or behaviors when you encounter them, whether in social settings, at work, or within your family.

Educate Others. Share what you've learned about systemic racism with friends, family and colleagues to foster a broader understanding.

Commit to Continuous Learning and Action. Keep up with current events and ongoing discussions about race and racism. Recognize that combating systemic racism is a long-term commitment. Continue to educate yourself, support initiatives and advocate for change even when it's challenging.

Form Meaningful Connections. Engage with people from different racial backgrounds to build understanding and empathy.

Community Involvement. Participate in community events and initiatives that promote racial harmony and understanding.

By taking these steps, White people can play a crucial role in dismantling systemic racism and building a more equitable society. Let's all do the "next right thing" to defeat systemic racism in all its forms.

Made in the USA
Columbia, SC
15 July 2024

dba72d17-b602-403a-a1df-59d7572b8586R01